STUDIES OF
ENGLISH POETS

STUDIES OF ENGLISH POETS

BY

J. W. MACKAIL

HONORARY FELLOW OF BALLIOL COLLEGE
FORMERLY PROFESSOR OF POETRY IN THE UNIVERSITY OF OXFORD

Essay Index Reprint Series

Originally published by:
LONGMANS, GREEN AND CO.

 BOOKS FOR LIBRARIES PRESS
FREEPORT, NEW YORK

First Published 1926
Reprinted 1968

Reprinted from a copy in the collections of
The Brooklyn Public Library

LIBRARY OF CONGRESS CATALOG CARD NUMBER:
68-25604

PRINTED IN THE UNITED STATES OF AMERICA

TO

W. P. KER

IN MEMORIAM

CONTENTS

INTRODUCTION

THE studies comprised in this volume range over a good many years in their original composition, and over portions of a large field in their subject. That field is indeed inexhaustible ; nor do these essays attempt to do more than indicate and exemplify lines of approach which may be of use for guidance or suggestion ; they may help, perhaps, towards appreciation of the attitude in which poetry may be read so as to be alive, and to communicate its vitalising quality. Their aim throughout has been, in the first place, to disengage the living and effective poetical value of the work of selected English poets, and, secondly, to bring that work into its place in the organic evolution of English poetry. In a previous volume, *The Springs of Helicon*, as indicated by the sub-title *A Study in the Progress of English Poetry from Chaucer to Milton*, this was the line of approach taken ; and it is retained here on different ground.

The best use, to be sure, that we can make of the poets is not to comment on them, but to read them. Much of what is called poetical criticism is obscuration of the poetry by the interposition of an opaque or distorting medium. Many biographical accounts of poets seem to throw light on anything but their poetry, and to divert attention from that by an irrelevant and (in the proper sense of the word) an extravagant curiosity. Textual study has its own separate value, which is always great and often highly illuminating. But commentary of whatever kind is only useful in so far as it throws light on the poetry itself and allows a more unimpeded access to it.

The studies collected here do not profess to present new facts, to embody the results of research, or to give a full account of the poets with whom they deal, but to place these poets in relation to the evolution of the art of which they are exponents. That art is a single though multiform process ; national in the sense of being a continuous product, and a progressive interpretation, of the imaginative energy of the nation, but linked also, as the nation itself is, to that wider human movement of which it is an organic element.

In order to do this, it is necessary to bring out, to the best of one's ability, the essential qualities of the poetry brought under review ; and in particular, the individual colour which a poet's own personality, acting upon and reacted upon by his own environment, gives to his poetry as seen in perspective and as it makes its appeal to the present time. In so far as a poet's work effectively survives, it represents the impact upon its readers' minds of a living force. Like life itself, it calls for and requires perpetual reinterpretation. There is no finality in the appreciation of poetry. If there were, the poetry would have ceased to live. This is true even of those classics, the product of a remote past and a foreign language, whose reputation is most consolidated and least subject to fluctuation of taste, of outlook, of intelligence. Still less can there be even an approximation to finality when the poets are those of our own race and the poetry is the utterance of our own speech.

It is this common method of approach which gives, as I venture to hope, a certain unity to the contents of the present volume. It is one method among others ; but the claim may be made for it that it leads more directly to the heart of poetry than either the technical analysis of style, language and metre, or the antiquarian investigation of actual or possible sources, or, what is perhaps more frequent, as it is more dangerous, the attempt to explain works of art by reducing them to the terms of some philosophic system or (in Pater's mordant phrase) some facile orthodoxy of our own.

The paper on Shakespeare, given as an inaugural address to a newly-founded English Association in one of our great Dominions, had for its object to suggest lines of enquiry which such an Association might be stimulated to pursue, and to emphasise certain facts to be borne in mind and certain mistakes to be avoided. It incorporated the greater part of the annual Shakespeare Lecture given to the British Academy on the occasion of the tercentenary of Shakespeare's death, as it was itself given in connexion with the like anniversary of the publication of the First Folio. After it comes a study of Sir Richard Fanshawe as an interesting figure and a significant landmark in the period of the transition, with its confused welter of poetical movements. The four studies which follow, on Pope, Thomson, Young, and Collins, are contributions offered towards a fuller and more just appreciation of the aims and effective achievements of English poetry in the eighteenth century. It had been my intention to carry this review further, and to trace, through similar studies among poets of the second half of the century, the organic movement, remarkable alike in its variety and its fertility, of that great germinal and constructive age. I have been unable to do so ; but I may be allowed to express the hope that other hands may take up and carry on this larger task.

The note on the composition of Keats' *Endymion* hardly, perhaps, comes within the general scope of the volume as indicated above. But I was reluctant—who would not be ?—to leave unmentioned in a volume dealing with the evolution of English poetry a poet whose greatness, not in mere promise (as has been said so often and with such imperfect appreciation) but in actual accomplishment, is being more and more largely realised. The studies of Morris and Swinburne require no explanatory comment. That of Tennyson is the main substance of lectures given in Adelaide, Sydney, and Brisbane at the invitation of the Australian Universities.

For permission to reprint matter already published I have to thank the Council of the British Academy, the Delegates of the Oxford University Press, the Syndics of the Cambridge University Press, and the Council of the Royal Society of Literature.

November 1925.

SHAKESPEARE

THE INAUGURAL ADDRESS TO THE AUSTRALIAN
ENGLISH ASSOCIATION, SYDNEY, 10 JULY 1923

SHAKESPEARE

My choice of subject for the Inaugural Address to this newly-founded Association, which it is my honour and privilege to give to-night, requires no explanation, still less any apology. To all the English-speaking world in both hemispheres, Shakespeare is central and vital; and in the activities of any English Association, here or elsewhere, the study of Shakespeare necessarily takes a commanding place.

But there is a further reason which makes the choice specially relevant to the occasion. This year is the ter-centenary of the publication of the famous First Folio, one of the two volumes which have during the last three hundred years most profoundly and continuously moulded English thought and national character, and which do so still, not only in the Mother Country but in the Dominions beyond the seas and in all the nations which share our blood and speech. For more than half of the whole body of the Shakespearian plays, the First Folio is our only source. Even for the others, we should be poorly off without it ; but without it, we should have lost irretrievably and totally such masterpieces as *Twelfth Night* and *As You Like It* in comedy, as *Macbeth* and *Antony and Cleopatra* in tragedy, as *A Winter's Tale* and *Cymbeline* in romance.

After three hundred years of familiarity, we are now only beginning to study and understand at all adequately

the contents of that priceless volume.   A revolution has
been wrought, in our own time, by the application to the
whole Elizabetho-Jacobean drama, and to Shakespeare in
particular, of the new armament of scholarship ; by that
pursuit of humane studies through scientific methods in
which the unity of learning declares itself and fulfils its
function.   Such study it will be one of the objects of
this Association to pursue and promote.

It is true that to read Shakespeare, not to read notes
or commentaries on Shakespeare, is what matters ; and
not only to read the plays, but to see and hear them acted;
for they are dramas for representation, not literary pieces.
In representation also they should be given as they are,
through a translucent medium ; not cut down and
mangled, not crushed by scenery, not distorted to suit
the vanity of actors or the caprice of stage managers.
Towards the attainment of this object likewise, the
Association may, and I hope will, give attention and
effort.   But it is no less true that we now can either read,
or hear and see, the plays with immensely increased dis-
crimination and intelligence because of the work, textual
and interpretative, which has been done on them by
modern scholarship ; by the application to Shakespeare,
that is, of those methods of research and criticism with
which we have long been familiar in the study of Greek or
Latin classics.   This work is being carried on with far-
reaching effects in the Mother Country and in America.
The Cambridge Shakespeare, a series in which six plays
have up to the present appeared, is invaluable alike for
the student and for the ordinary reader.   It rests with
this Association to further the pursuit of similarly illuminating study here.   The other day I had placed in my
hands the first volumes of an Australasian Shakespeare.
The names of the Editors guarantee the competence of

their work ; but its scope seems to be unfortunately contracted. The series is stated in the publishers' advertisement to be " the result of effort to provide sound school texts which will meet the requirements of the Examination Boards." This may be a necessary, or at least a defensible, object. But an Australasian Shakespeare worthy of the title will make a wider appeal in a larger and more humane spirit.

This is not an occasion for mere customary eulogy of the greatest name in English letters ; but rather for asking ourselves what Shakespeare really was, and what after three centuries he really is. For doing so the time is doubly apt. Industry and minute research have accumulated, one may say with some confidence, all the ascertainable facts which are of any importance, besides many more that are of none ; the material has been gathered, weighed and sorted for a constructive synthesis. And while no limit can be put to the concurrent process of appreciation or vital interpretation—for the secret of art is never to be won from her—yet even here we may stand back, and try to realise how, in effect, the matter stands.

" Let not my love be called idolatry," Shakespeare wrote in the *Sonnets*, " or my beloved as an idol shew." It is a counsel to be borne in mind. His canonisation had already begun when Jonson broke out into the petulant but not unreasonable protest, " I loved the man, and do honour his memory on this side idolatry as much as any." It had become a fixed and formulated doctrine within a century, when Pope, with a fine and discriminating touch, noted that " men of judgment think they do any man more service in praising him justly than lavishly." " Poets," he continues—and the words are an anticipatory sentence on much later Shakespearian criticism—" are always afraid of envy ; but sure they have as much reason to be afraid of admiration." " Idolatry of Shakespeare," Gibbon observed half a century later, " is inculcated from our infancy as the first duty of an Englishman." For a more familiar statement of the case we may turn to a well-known passage in *Mansfield Park*. " Shakespeare," says Henry Crawford, " one gets acquainted with without knowing how. It is part of an Englishman's constitution. His thoughts and beauties are so spread about that one touches them everywhere ; one is intimate with him by instinct."

That instinctive intimacy was no doubt rather superficial ; that simple-minded idolatry fell far short of real appreciation. To the orthodox enthusiasm of the eighteenth century there succeeded first the analysis of more fully equipped criticism, and then, close on its heels, the new idolatry of the romantic revival. That revival, like all revolutions, had been long prepared for, and, like all successful revolutions, resulted in something different from what its authors meant. Its results on Shakespeare were twofold. On the one hand it quickened interest, and opened out regions in his art which until then had been left unexplored. On the other hand it erected him into something supernaturally inspired, impeccable, omniscient. Behind Coleridge and Hazlitt came an army of prophets of their enthroned divinity. It was not sufficient that they should show Shakespeare to be, as he was, an adept in stagecraft, a master of language, the wielder of a versification unmatched for bright speed and supple strength. It was not sufficient that they should reaffirm him to be—the phrase is originally Pope's—" not so much an imitator as an instrument of nature." He must needs be also a profound thinker, a great moral and religious teacher, an author in whose works may be found the key to all problems and the quintessence of human or all but superhuman wisdom. Nothing less than universal knowledge, nothing short of a doctrine and a message on all matters which concern life was claimed for one who was assumed to be, in Coleridge's words, " myriad-minded," and " the guide and the pioneer of true philosophy." In him, as in a bible, all schools found what they sought.

The excess provoked its own reaction. Shakespeare the idol had swollen to such prodigious proportions that he began to topple over. Devotion stimulated research. Research raised doubts and started theories. The process of destructive criticism began. Under a misapplication of scientific method, the Shakespearian environment threatened to swamp Shakespeare. The invention of new criteria for determining authorship in writings of mixed composition led to the early vagaries of the New Shakspere Society. The width of knowledge assigned to him, or postulated of him, by his idolators created a school of theorists which still subsists, who, instead of examining the premises, swallowed them whole and drew from them a yet more preposterous conclusion.

Modern idolatry keeps breaking out in fresh forms, sometimes even more vagrant and fantastical. The illusion of reality in Shakespeare's characters is so powerful that they are thought of as existing outside of and apart from the plays themselves ; as though Shakespeare had suppressed or ignored or falsified material facts about them, as though the action in the plays were a fragment only of some larger whole which our superior insight enables us to reconstitute. Like conjectural emendations of a text based not on the enquiry what the author wrote, but on the speculation what he ought to have written, these theoretic extensions and reconstitutions offer a large playground. In early days, Fletcher wrote *The Tamer Tamed* as a continuation, or a rejoinder, to *The Taming of the Shrew*. A living author has written a play introducing a younger Lear and his wife, with Goneril as a girl. These are legitimate exercises of fancy. And there is no reason why anyone should not take one of Shakespeare's plays and make a better play of it—if he can. It was what Shakespeare himself habitually did with the plays of other dramatists. But to read a philosophy into his work, or to invent some " obsession " in him and hunt for traces of it throughout his plays, is not only idle but actively misleading.

To recall criticism from such extravagances, it is only necessary to notice facts about Shakespeare and about his age and environment. Such study is one of those which this Association may most usefully originate and promote.

The " spaciousness " of the Elizabethan age is largely an illusion. It was a period of material expansion and of intellectual activity, but it was also one of contraction, of low morality and debased art. Humanism had not struck deep root in England. The reformation carried out by the Tudor Monarchy, in the phrase of a fine historian, laid its foundations in the murder of the English Erasmus, and set up its gates in the blood of the English Petrarch. In the year when Shakespeare came to London, what was left of the English Renaissance died with Sidney. The provincial middle class to which Shakespeare belonged inherited, as they transmitted, the insular virtue of easy-going good temper, and the insular vices of grossness, slovenliness, and indolence. The first of the Shakespeares mentioned in records was hanged. The first mention of Shakespeare's own father is of his being fined for keeping a dunghill in front of his house, and the last, that he died intestate in a muddle of petty embarrassments. The child of a shiftless family in a decaying little country town might seem born to float with the stream.

In effect, he did so ; and in that lies the paradox, and in some sense the secret, of his unique achievement. From first to last he moves through life

> With such a careless force and forceless care
> As if that luck, in very spite of cunning,
> Bade him win all.

The stream on which he floated he took always at the flood. He fitted into his environment (to use the Homeric simile) like an onion into its coat, at every point in close touch and engagement, with no gap and with no friction. By native instinct he took the line of least resistance, adapting himself to fashion and circumstance with complete flexibility. When still a mere boy, he accepts, passively as it would seem, the marriage arranged for him by Anne Hathaway's family. Three years later, either having according to the gossiping tradition made Stratford for the moment too hot to hold him, or merely finding an opening before him in connection with the London playhouses, he slips away, leaving his " clog "— it is the word used by Autolycus of Perdita—behind. He launches on London life, and takes to it like a duck to water. The " moral incoherence " which has been noted in the Elizabethan drama was common to stage and audience. But among the theatrical profession it was accompanied by an amount of actual immorality which excused if it did not entirely justify the strictures of the Puritans and the repeated but quite ineffective attempts of the Privy Council to close the theatres altogether. The miserable end of Greene, the more tragic but not less squalid death of Marlowe a few months later, give a lurid register of the soil and atmosphere in which the Shakespearian drama came to being :

> Things outward
> Do draw the inward quality after them
> To suffer all alike.

In that turbid sea of life Shakespeare finds himself. He makes friends everywhere, among his fellow-craftsmen and among the frequenters of the theatre. He becomes the handy man of the company. He marks, copies, and improves upon all the devices of " these harlotry players " and of the playwrights who fed them with material. He assimilates whatever he sees or hears or touches, always ready to do anything, and always doing it well. Poetry was in fashion, and patronage was valuable ; so he writes *Venus and Adonis*, and dedicates it to the greatest of his great acquaintances, a dissolute young lord of nineteen. The theatres being closed for the plague, he uses his enforced holiday to follow up that adventure with *Lucrece*, but never afterwards in all his life publishes a line. Two months after his only son's death—an odd time for such a thing—he applies for a coat of arms, and next spring buys New Place. Presently the stream takes a new turn, and he with it ; he goes back to his professional work, not now as an assistant, but as a manager, for ten years more. Then he retires to the easy eventless life of Stratford, conforming to its ways as he had done to the ways of London. Puritanism was becoming a rising force there as elsewhere. John Hall, Susanna's husband, was a strong Puritan ; she adopted her husband's way of thinking, and there is clear evidence that Shakespeare himself at least acquiesced in it : " If I be drunk," one seems to hear him saying, " I'll be drunk with those that have the fear of God." But local chatter was not wholly silenced ; it breaks out in the loose gossip that " he died a Papist," and survives in the curiously sub-acid flavour of the lines inscribed long after on Susanna's tombstone alongside of his own :

> Witty above her sexe, but that's not all,
> Wise to salvation was good Mistris Hall ;
> Something of Shakespeare was in that, but this
> Wholy of him with whom she's now in blisse.

Shakespeare himself, the suggestion is, was not of the company. Susanna's defamation suit—which, to be sure, she won—was forgotten then, but into the inferences which may be drawn from the dates of her marriage and her daughter Elizabeth's birth there is no need to enquire curiously. Neither to that, nor to her sister Judith's hasty and irregular marriage just before Shakespeare's own death, is too much weight to be attached. But they show the family ending much as it began.

Chettle speaks aptly of his " facetious grace "—the word " facetious " then still retained its Latin sense of " delicate "—and the same note is struck in the " sweet Mr. Shakespeare" of *The Return from Parnassus*. The epithets " sweet," " pleasant," " gentle," habitually applied to him by his contemporaries, imply this flexibility of soft manners and far from rigid morals, as do the few anecdotes of him which have any claim to authenticity. They show him as one who was acquiescent and not assertive, who avoided dispute, who chose the easiest way. When called as witness in a suit over a friend's will, all his evidence is that he has no recollection on the point at issue. His help or advice is asked by fellow-townsmen in matters of taxation or enclosure, but there is nothing to show that either was effectively given. His recorded suits for recovery of small debts are mere matters of course. The provisions of his will, so eagerly scanned for clues, are in all respects perfectly normal. And this brings us up to a point which has been so far neglected or missed that it may give a shock if baldly stated. An artist of the last century, James Smetham, now forgotten or only remembered as a friend of Rossetti, stumbled in his simplicity on what had eluded wiser heads, and what would be thrust aside in anger or contempt by Shakespeare's idolators : " Shakespeare was like putty to everybody and everything : the willing slave, pulled out, patted down, squeezed anyhow, clay to every potter. But he knew by the plastic hand what the nature of the moulder was."

That is true ; and it is essential to true appreciation. At the touch of this thin shaft of light, the facts arrange themselves, the puzzle straightens itself out. One begins to see how it might be that in his lifetime he was classed as only one among others, and that his death—a thing that has often moved wonder—passed wholly unnoticed, and did not call forth, in that copiously elegiac age, a single line of elegy. He did not impress his contemporaries greatly. Very likely we also might find him quite unimpressive ; for he would not be occupied in impressing us. He would be doing something quite different : taking our impression. He had *le don terrible de la familiarité* : " every lane's end, every shop, church, session, hanging, yields a careful man work." Not a word, not a humour, not a quality, but he immediately took its impress. On that amazing sensitive-plate were recorded every lineament of body and mind, " all forms, all pressures past, that youth and observation copied there." In that even more amazing developing-room the records were put together, and were reeled out so as to give the vibrating effect of life, yet of a life swifter, tenser, more vivid than that of our own actual experience. At will he could set that film-world of impressions into movement, could make its figures speak, act, think or feel, exult or suffer, as though they were really alive.

Impartiality, the lofty ideal of the historian, was for such a faculty almost a matter of course. Nothing in Shakespeare is more remarkable than his conspicuous fairness to all his characters. He has no favourites ; he has, we may even say, no antipathies. That fairness, that clarity of representation, is the index partly of an indulgent temper, but more largely of a sensitiveness which is in touch with the whole of life, not intermittently but continuously ; of a dramatic power which never sleeps. His " attitude " towards his own creations—Shylock, for instance, or Falstaff—has been hotly debated. He has no attitude towards them. He gives us them for what they are ; with their virtues and vices, their strength and weakness, neither isolated nor commented on, but recorded. They must be taken as they are given. " Generally, in all shapes that man goes up and down in, from fourscore to thirteen, this spirit walks in." From fourscore to thirteen ; from Lear to Juliet ! The power to expatiate in that vast range is genius ; but part of the genius, what we may even call its central part, is boundless impressionableness, and a faculty as boundless for combining and reproducing impressions. We are hardly justified in saying that Shakespeare hates even his villains, or loves even his heroines. Lady Macbeth, the " fiend-like queen," may not be, what she has been called by a Shakespearian student of repute, "a sunny, bright, dainty little woman " : but she is, as Mr. Bradley justly points out, " up to her light, a perfect wife." The " delicate fiend," the Queen in *Cymbeline*, is, with the same reservation, a perfect mother. King John can retain to the end, treacherous and mean and cruel as he is, the absolute loyalty of Faulconbridge. Edmund was beloved. The one figure in the plays for whom Shakespeare shows something like antipathy is Iago ; and Iago is not quite a real person. " I am not what I am " are his own enigmatic but significant words.

Iago's words are the direct negative of what Shakespeare says of himself in a Sonnet which is admittedly autobiographical : " I am that I am." " There is no man hath a virtue that he hath not a glimpse of, nor any man an attaint but he carries some stain of it." To represent him otherwise is a pious fiction ; it must be discarded with those forms of idolatry which make him out a learned scholar, a trained lawyer, an expounder in dramatic allegories of the Platonic philosophy, or a profound political thinker. In all these and other matters he gives out the impressions made on him by the life about him. The only things of which we may say with some assurance that he had expert knowledge and real enjoyment are, on the one hand, field-sports, and on the other, the mechanism of the theatre and the technique of the actor and the playwright. His classical knowledge cannot be shown to have gone beyond Lily's Grammar and some scraps of Ovid. He had a little bad French, and a few words of Italian. His acquaintance with the Bible, on which volumes have been written for edification, is what he could not fail to pick up from the amount of church-attendance which was required by statute and enforced by sharp penalties. His painter in *Timon* (the opening scene of that play is his, not Chapman's nor another's) is brilliantly true to life ; but about painting he obviously knew little and cared less. Of music, from " Sneak's noise " to ditties

Sung by a fair queen in a summer's bower
With ravishing division to her lute,

he writes delightfully, but never like a musician. Legal phraseology, as was the habit of his age, he uses copiously, even to excess ; but his law, as distinct from this, is either taken direct from the novel or chronicle he was drama-tising, or is frank stage-law, poetical justice unknown to any court or code. Equally baseless is the assumption of his anti-democratic temper. In the follies of his mobs, as in the sarcasms of his aristocrats, he reflects the spirit of his audience whether at Whitehall or at the Bankside. No less, when in his later work, in *King Lear* and else-where, he sounds the note of passionate pity for the poor, is he giving out what he received ; it is his swift response to the ground-swell of the new democracy. Like the poet in *Timon*—a sketch as vivid as its companion-portrait of the painter—one seems to hear him say of his own work,

> A thing slipped idly from me :
> Our poesy is as a gum, which oozes
> From whence 'tis nourished.

Research has done away with the old careless belief that the body of work passing under Shakespeare's name is all his. Common sense rejects the more extravagant fancy that it embodies a system of human nature and a directory for human life. Yet that work in its massed total has another if a subtler kind of unity. The amount of non-Shakespearian work in what is called Shakespeare is large : alike in the earlier period when he was adapting and piecing out older men's plays, in the later period when younger men were doing the same with his, and even between the two, where the stage-text that has reached us was made up in a hurry by putting several hands to work on it, or has been altered for performance by stage-managers or by irresponsible actors. Kemp the comedian is said to have been turned out of the company at the Globe because he gagged to an extent beyond what the playwrights and his fellow actors could stand : and

this was just after he had made a great success in the
"creation," to use the modern slang, of Dogberry. How
much of our Dogberry is Shakespeare, how much Kemp ?
Macbeth has reached us in a mutilated form, with inter-
polations as we as cuts ; and whether the gag in the
famous scene of the knocking at the gate is Shakespeare's
own or not, or partly both, is a question which will always
be argued and will always have the interest of being in-
soluble. The unity of Shakespeare is that of the Shakespearian touch, the Shakespearian inspiration, which
spreads through and vivifies all the work he laid his finger
upon. Hence, to borrow a phrase from another art, the
flooding of his colour in composite work. Between what
is pure Shakespeare and what is wholly non-Shakespearian, the difference is as obvious as it is profound.
But who will undertake to say confidently whether we
are faced, in parts of *2 Henry VI*, with Marlowe filled in
by Shakespeare, or Shakespeare writing like Marlowe, as
he still did in *King John* ; in parts of *Henry VIII*, with
Fletcher writing (as nearly as he could) like Shakespeare,
or Shakespeare writing (as he easily could if he chose)
like Fletcher ? A few touches of the master-hand have
worked wonders in the coarse and repulsive tragedy of
Titus Andronicus. No other dramatist of the age had that
flooding and irradiating power. When they collaborated
hey either mixed mechanically, or combined, at best, into
something which does not bear the impress of a single
welding and controlling genius.

Appreciation comes of comprehension. We can best
honour, as we can only appreciate, Shakespeare by reading
him. This is not a portentous platitude ; for it is what
few do. We all read in him, which is a different thing ;
we most of us read into him, which is a different thing
again. and a more dangerous one. No one has begun to

understand Shakespeare who has not read the plays as a whole, as a single body of work. Needless difficulties have been put in the way of doing so by the artificial disorder in which, ever since their first collection, they have been arranged. He loses by this much as the Old and New Testament do ; at least it would be so if people read, as they seldom read, either the Bible or Shakespeare straight through. But they would be more likely to do that, and would do it with fresh understanding, were both volumes not set out with almost heroic disregard of chronological order. It is worth while pausing here to consider this.

The precise dates, the true order of the plays, are not indeed fully ascertainable. Groups overlap ; the place of a particular play in its group is often uncertain ; and with those which were repeatedly recast and revised for later performance, it may be arguable whether to place them, in the form in which they have reached us, at an earlier or later point in the list. But with these reservations, and subject to a margin of error which is not great, it is possible to read the plays through in the order of their composition ; and to do so opens Shakespeare out like a new world. Planes come out, lines of growth tell, methods reveal themselves. We get solid footing ; we realise his organic continuity. It is

> a course more promising
> Than a wild dedication of yourselves
> To unpath'd waters, undream'd shores :

nor, voyaged over with chart and compass, do shores or waters lose anything of their marvel and richness.

The four earliest plays are trial-pieces ; experiments in four different dramatic forms, on three at least of which, if not on all four, he spent much labour in careful revision. He begins with the " literary " drama of criticism and

C

satire in *Love's Labour's Lost*, then takes up romantic comedy in *The Two Gentlemen*, romantic tragedy in *Romeo and Juliet*, and traditional Plautine comedy in the *Comedy of Errors*. After thus feeling his way, mastering his mechanism, and proving his competence, he works mainly on English history-plays for the new Rose Theatre for about three years. First he adapts and revises plays already produced, remodelling Peele and Greene, collaborating with Marlowe ; then entirely rewrites an older *King John*, and carries forward the series unassisted in *Richard II*, and probably in collaboration, in *Richard III*. Next, letting loose as it were the accumulated pressure of romantic imagination, he flowers out into the loveliest and most exquisitely finished of all poetic romances, wholly his own both in invention and in execution, *A Midsummer Night's Dream*.

After some light work in comedy, a marked break follows, the only one in the twenty years of his dramatic activity. Then he resumes English history in the double play of *Henry IV*, with a new richness and amplitude. The Globe Theatre is built, and he becomes a full partner in the ownership and management. For its opening season he writes the great spectacular history of *Henry V*, and follows it up with the three central comedies, *As You Like It*, *Much Ado*, *Twelfth Night*, the flower and crown of the English drama, all produced, with incredible speed, in little more than a year. He was then thirty-five; it is the *annus mirabilis* of his life, and of the English stage.

Then he makes a swift transition.

> He was dispos'd to mirth, but on the sudden
> A Roman thought hath struck him,

and with *Julius Caesar* he opens the period of the great tragedies. They were written for what had become a more educated, more intelligent, probably more exacting audience ; and more particularly, for production before a Court which, in a time empty of political events, was giving not only patronage but serious attention to the drama. " These three years," he makes Hamlet say in 1602, " I have taken note of it, the age is grown so picked that the toe of the peasant comes near the heel of the courtier" : and the courtier (as in *Hamlet*) was imposing his own choice of treatment on the playwright. Shakespeare moved on the crest of the wave. *Hamlet* is not only a tremendous reaction from *Twelfth Night*, it is the recognition of a new age with new requirements. *Troilus and Cressida* (however much or however little of it be Shakespeare's, and much more of it is his than modern critics are disposed to admit) is the by-product or backwash of that gigantic achievement, as a few years earlier *The Merry Wives* had been of *Henry IV*, as a few years later *Timon* is of *King Lear*.

The new reign carried the movement forward. The " princely " drama of Beaumont shows the culmination of the influence to which Shakespeare had already fully responded when *Othello*, *Macbeth*, and *King Lear* were produced before the Court at Whitehall. In the superdrama—a name applicable here if anywhere—of *Antony and Cleopatra*, tragedy is expanding into something beyond itself. We are on the brink of a new dramatic revolution. But within the same year, *Philaster* took the world captive by a fresh and enchanting dramatic method. After it, Shakespeare writes no more tragedies.

The vogue of Beaumont's great colleague had then begun. To Fletcher's agile, flexible workmanship Shakespeare shows none of the jealousy of an older artist, none of that suspicion of new methods which is so common among writers of established position. He responds to this influence as to others.   In the opening scene of *Coriolanus* there are traces of Fletcher's manner, if not of his actual hand.   When Shakespeare retired, Fletcher formally succeeded him as head dramatist of the company. The brief age of high concentration was over.   In twenty years the English drama passed from the fiery dawn of Marlowe to the silvered dusk of Massinger.   The interval was its day ; it was the day of Shakespeare.   Before it faded away into the comedy of manners and the tragedy of sentiment, it had put out new growths : for Court representations, the masque ; for popular audiences, loosely woven melodramatic romance.   This change of current also Shakespeare followed before he quitted the theatre for good.   He put seven scenes of his own very finest work into *Pericles*, an artless and ill-written chronicle-romance by a hack writer.   He produced, in *Cymbeline* and *The Winter's Tale*, two exquisite romances of his own, adapting for the latter the sketch of a tragedy perhaps already composed.   In *The Tempest* he recognised and as it were sanctioned the masque before he finally gave the reins of dramatic control into the hands of the After-born.

His own last appearance on the stage is believed to have been in this piece.   In the epilogue to it, which, though spoken by Prospero, is not part of the play and is not necessarily dramatic, we seem for once to hear Shakespeare's own voice, the voice of one making his final acquiescence :

Now my charms are all o'erthrown
And what strength I have's my own,
Which is most faint.   Now I want
Spirits to enforce, art to enchant.

" We are Time's subjects, and time bids begone."   The lines may be set beside and balanced against what is the

earliest extant piece of Shakespeare's writing, the opening
words of *Love's Labour's Lost* :

> Let fame, that all hunt after in their lives,
> Live registered upon our brazen tombs
> And then grace us in the disgrace of death.

It is tempting to read into these lines a preluding trumpet-
flourish of his own young ambition ; but though tempting, unjustified.   They are Shakespeare catching and
repeating (yet repeating, as always, with a difference) the
accent of Marlowe.   But the fame that was in his own
mind was likely, at the time, less that to be gained by
" still climbing after knowledge infinite " than the more
obvious glory of Tamburlaine's copper-laced coat and
crimson velvet breeches—one of the earliest sights to
dazzle his eyes when he came to London.   The *Sonnets*
show him wincing under the soilure of an actor's profession, yet realising that all fame, great and small, is
alike transitory, and

> lays great bases for eternity
> Which prove more short than waste or ruining.

From the early days when he was

> Like one that stands upon a promontory
> And spies a far-off shore where he would tread

until the end, we seem to hear him saying

> On :
> Things that are past are done with me :

and if he dallied with the fancy that

> Time, with his fairer hand
> Offering the fortunes of his former days,
> The former man may make him,

he was surely too cognisant of life to dream of any Medea's
magic that " embalms and spices to the April-day again."

From first to last Shakespeare is not an inventor or innovator. He follows the stream of inventions and innovations, takes them up, puts into them his own mastery of technique, his own incomparable dexterity, his own vitality. It is the same with his poems. *Venus and Adonis* is modelled on Lodge ; *Lucrece*, even more closely, on Daniel. The *Sonnets* were in any case composed after the Sonnet-sequence had become fashionable, and according to what is the more probable view, after that fashion had passed its climax and was fading. In the management of metre indeed, in his handling of the flexible dramatic blank verse, he explored as well as perfected. The secret of his later versification remains his, and all attempts to recapture it have been vain. His prose too, is his own creation. Otherwise, it is almost as though he deliberately refused to make new experiments of his own. What was about him, in art as in life, was good enough for him.

Sufflaminandus erat (" the brake had to be put on him ") is Jonson's remark on Shakespeare's unequalled fluency. " Faster than spring-time showers comes thought on thought," and the expression never lags behind. Words were with him like persons and things ; none escaped his notice, none failed to make their impression on him, none slipped his memory. His vocabulary still remains the largest of any English author ; in light or in grave use, he pours it out with equally facile mastery.

And so, when he puts the brake on, he can concentrate this power, and charge his language with all the accumulated force that he holds in reserve. "No other man could so strike with words." In many such strokes— from the awful " And Cassandra laughed " of Pandarus to Albany's soundless " Even so : cover their faces," or the whisper of Imogen " I hope I dream," a few words of extreme simplicity carry in them an unequalled sense of vastness, an all but intolerable poignancy.

Shakespeare's flexibility in the use of language is nowhere more striking than in its self-adjustment to light or serious purposes with equal certainty. This applies alike to form and to substance. His verse is so supple, his prose so musical and vibrating, that they mingle and flood ; it is often a matter of doubt whether a speech, or a whole scene, is in rhythmic prose or free verse, and decision between the two is hardly more than an accident of printing. But similarly, the same language carries with it, often with all but verbal identity, the extremes of mirth or terror. The senile babble of Shallow, " I have lived fourscore years and upward. . . . I have seen the time with my long sword I would have made you four tall fellows skip like rats," reappears in the piteous accent of Lear :

> I am a very foolish fond old man
> Fourscore and upward. . . .
> I have seen the day, with my good biting falchion,
> I would have made them skip.

Macbeth's tragic utterance of self-torture,

> Had I but died an hour before this chance
> I had lived a blessed time,

is repeated as a mere light romantic thrill in the Old Shepherd of Bohemia's

> If I might die within this hour, I have lived
> To die when I desire.

The essences of comedy and tragedy themselves are summed in Feste's words, " And thus the whirligig of time brings in his revenges," and those of Edmund,

> The wheel is come full circle : I am here.

" His mind and hand went together," Shakespeare's colleagues wrote of him just three hundred years ago. But no hand, not even his, could keep abreast of his swift envisagement of dramatic action, or of the crowd of words that rushed to express it. More and more, as he goes on, one sees him, if not unable, at least too impatient to deploy his forces. Language poured in on him faster than he could put it down, and he came more and more " to crash through it like a thunderbolt," one thought or image treading so hard on the heels of another that they became merged or fused. Just the same thing happened to his versification. The metrical pattern is always there, but as the loom flies it is crushed into vast deviations. Many passages in which we still feel the metrical structure can only be printed as prose, because the rhythms have outrun the framework, and got quite beyond the compass of the pattern. But in the most irregular the sense of pattern is not lost, it only is submerged and re-emerges. Both as regards thought and words he gives the impression of the whole content of a speech or a scene rising in his mind together, and of his getting down on paper as much of it as he can, in what order and form he can. His apprehensions are simultaneous, not consecutive. And this applies to the action as well as to the language of the plays. Only one or two, and none of the later plays, give the impression of having been composed from a scenario. The action seems to rise before him as a single complex whole. In translating this into concrete actable form, he is obliged to sort it out into sequence ; but he does not aim at more than dramatic coherence, than the degree of consecutiveness that satisfies an audience. If analysed further, the action in the plays presents gaps, inconsistencies, sometimes impossibilities. That he left it so was from no deep plan. It is not merely idle, it is actively misleading, to argue or infer what happens outside of what is shown happening, as though the picture went on behind the frame, or as though the actors continued to act after they step off the stage.   Yet art here once more triumphantly justifies the artist.   It is just this massed, partially incoherent treatment which keeps his plays from suggesting mechanism and makes them so true an image of life.   The vague dissatisfaction left (as its best admirers have allowed) by *As You Like It* is due less to any tangible flaw than to a subconscious impression of artificial flaw-lessness.   The inconsistencies which no ingenuity can explain away in *Othello* or *Hamlet* give to these plays no slight part of their arresting and compelling power.   They give, in a way that no other dramatist (unless it be Sophocles) has ever equalled, the awful and enigmatic quality of life.   They keep us from " ensconcing our-selves into seeming knowledge, when we should submit ourselves to an unknown fear."

Let me add a word on two points often missed or denied, but essential to true appreciation.

Shakespeare is not a moral teacher.   He lets morality take care of itself; what he sets before us is life.   Cruelty, falsehood, lust, treachery are represented by him, as are heroism, truth, self-sacrifice ; but they are neither ap-proved nor condemned, they are only displayed, as causes with their effects, or it may be with their strange apparent effectlessness.   Lady Capulet's plan to have Romeo poisoned in Mantua, Cymbeline's order for the massacre in cold blood of all his Roman prisoners, are presented without comment, and come to no result.   The lesson, if it can be called one, of Shakespeare, as of Sophocles, is that we should not draw lessons, but see and feel and understand.   Their attitude towards the virtues is that they are virtues, that good is different from evil.   If it be part of the scheme of things (as does not always appear) that there is a Power which works for righteousness, that is only one fact like others.   Shakespeare does not teach ; he illuminates.   In his clear daylight we see the world. The exaltation with which even his darkest tragedies leave us comes of our having, through him, seen it as it is, neither good nor bad in any strict meaning, but wonderful.   Goneril and Cordelia, Iago and Othello, are alike parts of life :   " he maketh his sun to rise on the evil and on the good, and sendeth rain on the just and on the unjust."   And it is not the lesson of Shakespeare, but the lesson of life, borne in upon us through that image of life which Shakespeare holds up before us, that good is not only different from evil, but better than evil.

Nor, any more than he is a teacher of morals, is Shakespeare a teacher of patriotism.   The love and praise of England which he makes his great Englishmen utter are theirs, not his ;   only he makes them express themselves as none but he could do.   In clearing our minds of idolatry, we must take into account not such passages only, too familiar for citation, too august for praise,

> England, hedged in with the main,
> That water-walled bulwark, still secure
> And confident from foreign purposes :
>
> This England never did nor never shall
> Lie at the proud foot of a conqueror :
>
> This royal throne of kings, this scepter'd isle,
> England, bound in with the triumphant sea :

not only these, but the representations, equally sympathetic because equally dramatic, of the merely vulgar attitude of mind towards the native country, and of the narrow, insular prejudice against foreigners ; the swagger about the boy (not yet born) "that shall go to Constantinople and take the Turk by the beard," and the ignorant conceit which sets down all Frenchmen as braggarts, all Germans as sots, and all Italians as fiends. Once more here, Shakespeare does not teach ; he illuminates. He shows us that patriotism is not only different from, but better than, want of patriotism. He does not teach this as a lesson ; he presents it as a fact.

And in the lessons, if we will call them so, or the facts of life, the ultimate and central fact is its power of self-renewal :

> If the ill spirit have so fair a house,
> Good things will strive to dwell with 't.

To the lips of each new generation comes the ecstatic cry,

> O wonder !
> How many goodly creatures are there here !
> How beauteous mankind is ! O brave new world
> That has such people in 't !

and the older generation may realise this, and may answer, as Prospero does to Miranda, with no accent of sadness or of sarcasm, with no trace even of superior indulgence, but with full thankfulness,

> 'Tis new to thee.

Perhaps, when all is said, attempts to clarify our judgment, to dismiss and cancel outworn idolatries, only leave us established in some new idolatry of our own. They leave us, at all events, with a feeling for Shakespeare little short of adoration. Our predecessors of the last three hundred years often praised him, as they sometimes blamed him, amiss :

> Cats, that can judge as fitly of his worth
> As I can of these mysteries which heaven
> Will not have earth to know.

The mistake to which we, like them, are liable is to praise

him at all.   No words said of him are more exactly true than those of one who, in the last generation, was his most impassioned lover and most eloquent interpreter. After exhausting on Shakespeare all hyperboles of laudation, all glitter and pomp of rhetoric, Swinburne, as a poet and not as a panegyrist, wrote of him more simply what is the last and the unsurpassable word :

His praise is this, he can be praised of none.
Man, woman, child, praise God for him ; but he
Exults not to be worshipped, but to be.
He is ; and being, beholds his work well done.

SIR RICHARD FANSHAWE

A Lecture given at the Royal Society of
Literature, 25 March 1908

SIR RICHARD FANSHAWE

JUST one hundred years ago, Scott, writing to Miss Seward, slipped into a characteristic passage of his large, careless, human criticism. " Dryden's fame," he wrote, " has nodded, and that of Pope begins to be drowsy ; Chaucer is as sound as a top, and Spenser is snoring in the midst of his commentators. Milton indeed is quite awake, but observe, he was at his very outset refreshed with a nap of half a century ; and in the midst of all this, we sons of degeneracy talk of immortality."

In a world where such lapses into oblivion come over even the greatest names, the minor immortality attained by the second rank among men of letters is even fainter and more precarious. The name of Sir Richard Fanshawe is now little known except among professed students of the history and literature of the seventeenth century. But it is one which had an important place both in public life and in the development of English poetry ; and if it is necessary to introduce him to a modern audience by giving a brief sketch of his life, it is no waste of time to do so : for it was a life full of action and incident, and has been recorded for us by a loving hand in one of the most fascinating of biographies.

To the eighteenth century Fanshawe was superficially known, both as a statesman through the pages of Clarendon, and as a man of letters who was of some account in that period of transition which connects the age of the later Elizabethans with the age of Dryden. To Dryden himself and to Dryden's contemporaries, the generation which immediately succeeded his own, he had been a considerable figure. In the age which followed, the age of Pope and fully developed classicism, he shared the general neglect which overtook the English poets of the transition. His translation of the *Lusiads* of Camoens retained some position as a work which, though it had become obsolete, was still a sort of classic. Voltaire read it when he was in England between 1726 and 1729, and based upon it his slight and ill-informed criticism on Camoens, whom he had not read in the original, in his " Essay on the Epic Poetry of the European Nations." Fifty years later, Johnson, in his life of Dryden, mentions him, along with Denham, Waller, and Cowley, as one of the pioneers in the art of translation who " broke the shackles of verbal interpretation and showed the way towards elegance and liberty." Johnson's reading in older English literature was extensive though desultory. But probably he owed his acquaintance with Fanshawe to the extracts printed by Mickle a few years before in his own version of the *Lusiads*. After this, little attention was paid to Fanshawe for half a century.

All this while, the memoirs of Lady Fanshawe had remained in the obscurity of their original MS., which had fortunately remained intact, except for the loss of a few pages at the end, in the possession of the family. They gradually became known among antiquarians. The earliest allusion to them which has been traced is in the *Gentleman's Magazine* in 1787. About the same time Horace Walpole had been shown them, and found them " not unentertaining." Extracts from them, which after this were given from time to time in literary collections of anecdota or in county histories, began to rouse a keener interest in them ; and in 1829 they were published, with a preface and notes by Sir Harris Nicolas. That volume went into a second edition in the following year, but it seems probable that neither edition was large, and the memoirs remained but little known. They were not reprinted again until 1905. For many years before that, copies of the earlier editions could easily be picked up at a moderate price, as they still can be, by anyone who cared to look for them.

Meanwhile, however, the love of letters for which Sir Richard Fanshawe was so conspicuous had reappeared in the family. Sir Richard's own family, so far at least as male issue is concerned, became extinct in the next generation. But Mr. H. C. Fanshawe, the ninth in direct descent from Sir Richard's grandfather, has recently re-edited the memoirs from the original MS.—the earlier editions were all from a rather incorrect transcript made in 1766. He has also supplied them, in the exercise of a piety and industry which are as rare as they are commendable, with a complete body of illustrative collateral information. This definitive edition of the " Memoirs of Ann Lady Fanshawe " is a book which is delightful to possess, and for which much gratitude is due to its editor.

It is in the picture they give of Lady Fanshawe herself that the intimate charm of these memoirs lies. They were written in her widowhood, in order to preserve a memory for her only surviving son of the husband whom she had idolised. Love supplied for her all defects of skill. There is no fine writing in the memoirs, and no self-consciousness. The spirit in which she wrote may best be indicated by a few of her own words : " We never had but one mind throughout our lives. Our souls were wrapped up in each other, our aims and designs one, our loves one and our resentments one. Whatever was real happiness, God gave it me in him." The temptation to linger over her is great. But it is of Sir Richard himself, and of Sir Richard as a poet and man of letters, that I have undertaken to give some account. It will not be amiss to begin by giving the briefest possible outline of his life.

Richard Fanshawe was born in 1608, and was the fifth son of Sir Henry Fanshawe, of Ware Park, in Hertfordshire, Remembrancer of the Exchequer. This office was for a century and a half almost an appanage of the family ; no less than nine Fanshawes successively held it between the reign of Elizabeth and that of George I. Like many high officials of his time, Sir Henry was a scholar and a musician. The house and garden at Ware Park were both famous in an age of splendid domestic architecture and of sumptuous gardens such as are described in Bacon's essay. Here Richard Fanshawe lived until he was sent to Farnaby's famous school in Cripplegate, the Eton of the period. From it he proceeded to Jesus College, Cambridge, at the age of fifteen, and after finishing his course at the University, returned to London, and was entered as a student of the Inner Temple. Both at school and at college his orbit nearly intersected that of the most illustrious of his contemporaries. Milton, born a few months after Fanshawe, was at school at St. Paul's within half a mile of him, and entered Christ's the year after Fanshawe went to Jesus. The two, one fancies, must have met at Cambridge. Thenceforward their paths lay far apart. Milton remained at Cambridge for eight years, and was then buried for five or six years more in the seclusion of Horton; he started on his grand tour to Italy just about the time when Fanshawe returned from prolonged continental travel ; and after this Fanshawe was engaged in public affairs as an ardent Royalist, and could have little intercourse with men of letters belonging to the opposite party. It is, however, one of the curious freaks of history that at the Restoration Fanshawe succeeded Milton as Latin Secretary, and the conjecture has been hazarded that his influence may have helped towards the remarkable leniency with which the republican extremist and official defender of regicide was treated by the Restoration Government.

Between 1632 and 1638 Fanshawe was much abroad, in France, Italy, and Spain. He was for a time Secretary to the English Embassy at Madrid, and on his return was made Secretary to the Irish Council of War under Strafford. In November 1640 the Long Parliament met, and within a week had ordered Strafford's arrest. The Civil War broke out in 1642, and in the following spring Fanshawe joined the King at Oxford. From this time forward he was engaged incessantly in the Royal service.

Among the Royalists who were then crowding into Oxford from all quarters were the Harrisons, a Hertfordshire family, connected by marriage as well as by neighbourhood with the Fanshawes. The mother was dead, and the younger children were in the charge of the eldest daughter, Anne, a handsome and high-spirited girl of eighteen. It seems to have been a case of love at first sight on both sides ; but as to this, Lady Fanshawe, who, though as frank and free-spoken as one of Shakespeare's women, knows when to be reticent, says nothing. It was no easy time for marrying or giving in marriage. First, Anne's brother, William Harrison, hurt in a skirmish near Oxford, died of his wounds ; then

Fanshawe's appointment as Envoy to the Court of Denmark was actually made out, but afterwards cancelled. The estates of both families had been sequestrated by the Parliament, and they were all but penniless : " the stock we set up our trading with," Lady Fanshawe says, " did not amount to twenty pounds betwixt us " ; and Charles paid his servants with promises, not in cash. But in May 1644 they were married in the little church of Woolvercot, close to Oxford, and the long joint romance of their life began.

For its details one must go to the " Memoirs " themselves : it is a fascinating story, which during the next seven years ranges through England, Scotland, Ireland, France, Holland, and Spain ; a life of war and wandering, of shipwrecks, imprisonments, and hairbreadth escapes, borne in cheerful poverty and unconquerable loyalty. During the remainder of the Civil War Fanshawe held, successively, the offices of Secretary at War to Prince Charles, Treasurer of the Navy, Envoy Extraordinary to Spain, and Clerk of the Council and Secretary of State. In 1650 he was made a Baronet ; in the following year he was taken prisoner a few days after the battle of Worcester, and kept under close arrest in London for two months. It is of this imprisonment that Lady Fanshawe gives the vivid little picture which is perhaps the best known single passage in the " Memoirs":

Order came to carry him to Whitehall, where in a little room, yet standing in the bowling green, he was kept prisoner without the speech of any one, so far as they knew, ten weeks, and in expectation of death. They often examined him, and at last he grew so ill in health by the cold and hard marches he had undergone, and being pent up in a room close and small, that the scurvy brought him almost to death's door. During this time of his imprisonment I failed not constantly to go, when the clock struck four in the morning, with a dark lantern in my hand, all alone and on foot, from my lodging in Chancery Lane, at my cousin Young's, to Whitehall, at the entry that went out of King's Street into the bowling ground. There I would go under his window and softly call him. He that after the first time expected me, never failed to put out his head at first call. Thus we talked together ; and sometimes I was so wet with rain that it went in at my neck and out at my heels.

Cromwell had not only a respect, but a genuine liking for Fanshawe ; he " would have bought him off to his service at any terms," Lady Fanshawe says ; and when his overtures met with no acceptance, he arranged terms for him which were easy, and even, as things went, generous. His property remained in sequestration, but for the next seven years he was allowed to live in England wherever he chose free from any surveillance or molestation. It was in these seven years that most of his work in letters was done. Though thrust early into public affairs by inherited position, he was by nature a scholar and student rather than a man of action : he was happy so long as he had his wife and his books. " Pens, ink and paper was your father's trade," Lady Fanshawe tells her son. Herself high-spirited, active, and a fearless horsewoman, she seems now and then to have been inclined to complain of her husband's devotion to study, except that nothing that he did could be wrong. " He never used exercise but walking," she tells us, " and that generally with some book in his hand, which oftentimes was poetry." In October 1648 two Dutch ships fired on them when they were walking on the beach near Portsmouth. " He altered not his pace, saying, If we must be killed, it were as good to be killed walking as running."

At this point, therefore, it will be convenient to give some account of his published writings, among which it is not necessary for this purpose to include his letters and dispatches. He published but little original poetry, and does not seem to have written much. The bulk of his poetry, and that by which he obtained his reputation and his place in English literature, consists of translations from Latin, Italian, Spanish, and Portuguese. In all these languages he was an accomplished scholar. His earliest volume, a translation of the *Pastor Fido*, to which were annexed a few graceful original pieces, appeared in 1647, in the interval between the first and second Civil Wars, while Charles I was a prisoner at Holmby House, and terms of accommodation between him and the Parliament were under discussion. Guarini's famous pastoral play had appeared more than fifty years before, but it still remained at the height of its immense reputation throughout Europe. The English version by Dymock had been published as early as 1602, and had supplied the model and much of the inspiration for Fletcher's *Faithful Shepherdess* (? 1609). Fanshawe's own translation, which was dedicated to Prince Charles, was reprinted in the following year, and passed through five editions before the demand for it was exhausted. In the reprint of 1648 there was added to the volume a translation of the fourth book of the *Aeneid* in Spenserian verse.

The first-fruits of Fanshawe's forced retirement was a little volume of translations from Horace's Odes, published in 1651. For some considerable time afterwards he was engaged on his largest work in poetry, the translation of Camoens' *Lusiads*, in the *ottava rima* of the original. This appeared in 1655, and took its place as a standard work alongside of Fairfax's *Tasso*. Three years later was published the most curious of all his works and one very characteristic of the period, a translation into Latin verse of Fletcher's *Faithful*

Shepherdess. At the end of this volume mention is made of another work as yet unpublished (it was not, in fact, printed until after Fanshawe's death). This was a translation of a Spanish comedy, or rather masque, entitled *To Love only for Love's Sake* (" *Querer por solo Querer* "), by Antonio de Mendoza ; the date of the original in this case is 1623, and a dedication of the translation to Queen Christina of Sweden, presumably written soon after the translation was made and when Fanshawe meant to print it, is dated July 1654. This item may conclude our list ; there are some other occasional poems and translations to be recorded in a full bibliography of Fanshawe's works, but they need not detain us here. With the volume of 1658 Fanshawe's work in poetry ends.

The remainder of his life was a period of resumed and engrossing public employment. The *Fida Pastora* was entered for publication in March 1658. On September 3rd of that year Cromwell died, and three weeks later a pass was granted by the new Government to Fanshawe to go abroad. He rejoined Charles II at Paris, and was with him there and in the Low Countries and Holland until the Restoration. In January 1660 he was appointed Latin Secretary and Master of Requests; he crossed from Scheveling in the King's ship in May, and entered London with him ; soon after he was made Chancellor of the Order of the Garter, and was chosen member for the University of Cambridge in the Cavalier Parliament. In the autumn of 1661 he went as Envoy Extraordinary to Lisbon to complete the arrangements for the Portuguese match ; did the translator of Camoens, one must needs wonder, have any augury in his mind of how the insignificant island off the Indian coast, which Catharine of Braganza brought as part of her dowry, was to be the germ of an empire that should far eclipse that founded by Vasco da Gama and Affonso d'Albuquerque ? He returned to Lisbon as English Ambassador after the royal marriage, and after an interval at home, during which he was sworn of the Privy Council, sailed from Portsmouth at the beginning of 1664 as Ambassador to Spain. His special business there was the negotiation of a treaty. Things went amiss ; he was not supported properly by his own Government, and Lady Fanshawe hints at jealousies on the part of Clarendon. According to Pepys, Fanshawe was displaced in order to make room for the appointment of Sandwich, who had to be hustled away to screen the scandal over his embezzlement of the contents of captured Dutch ships. At all events Fanshawe was recalled in May 1666, and died of fever at Madrid in June as he was preparing to return to England. His illness was, no doubt, aggravated by vexation. The profligacy of the court and the want of principle in the Government were alike distasteful to him. On her way home with her husband's body, Lady Fanshawe received at Bilbao the news of the burning of London. It must have seemed to many of his friends that he had been taken away timely from the evil to come.

It was the end of an age and the beginning of another in literature as well as in public affairs. Fanshawe belonged to the period and school in poetry of the transition, of the later Jacobeans and earlier Carolines. He just missed seeing its extinction. In the year after his death Dryden's *Annus Mirabilis* and Milton's *Paradise Lost* were published ; and a new age began.

Milton and Fanshawe were, as I mentioned, exact contemporaries. Both received, at school and at the University, the elaborate classical education of that period ;

both supplemented it by further prolonged study, by large reading among the English and Italian poets, and by residence abroad in the company of foreign men of letters and scholars. It is a curious little fact that Fanshawe's Latin dedication to the Queen of Sweden, which I have already mentioned, coincides rather closely in substance, and even in language, with portions of Milton's semi-official eulogy of Christina in the *Defensio Secunda pro Populo Anglicano*, published two months earlier. But in poetry, almost from the first, the two give the impression not only of a different school and manner but almost of a different period. The difference is like that between Jacobean and Palladian architecture, which also overlap in this age ; the one continuing the Elizabethan tradition, richly ornamented, profuse, highly coloured, the other magnificent and austere. Fanshawe was by nature, and in spite of his scholarship and classical training, a romanticist ; Milton, even in the earlier poems in which the romantic influence is still strong, is the first and the greatest of the classicists.

There happens to be a single instance in which the two methods, and the whole difference in the technical quality of poetry that they involve, can be set side by side. Both Milton and Fanshawe translated the fifth ode of the first book of Horace. The precise date of the translation is not known in either case, but it is not very material. Milton's well-known version was first published among the additions made to the volume of his Poems when it was reprinted in 1673. These additions comprise pieces written both before and after the date of the original volume ; this piece comes between the Vacation Exercise of 1627 or 1628 and the Tetrachordon sonnet of 1645 or 1646, but it may be conjecturally dated later than both, and somewhere about

1650, which is also the date of Marvell's Horatian Ode on Cromwell's return from Ireland. A brief prefatory note to it contains the first hint of the thesis afterwards expanded by him in the preface to the *Paradise Lost*, that rhyme, " the jingling sound of like endings," was not merely " no necessary adjunct or true ornament of good verse," but " a thing of itself trivial and of no true musical delight," and that the neglect of rhyme was, therefore, " so little to be taken for a defect, though it may seem so perhaps to vulgar readers, that it rather is to be esteemed an example set of ancient liberty recovered from troublesome and modern bondage."

Fanshawe's Horace was published, as we have seen, in 1651. Let me quote the two renderings ; they will by themselves enforce the point which I wish to bring out better than can be done by any comment. Milton's, of course, takes place of the other :

> What slender Youth bedew'd with liquid odours
> Courts thee on Roses in some pleasant Cave,
>   *Pyrrha* for whom bind'st thou
>   In wreaths thy golden Hair,
> Plain in thy neatness ; O how oft shall he
> On Faith and changed Gods complain : and Seas
>   Rough with black winds and storms
>   Unwonted shall admire :
> Who now enjoyes thee credulous, all Gold,
> Who alwayes vacant, alwayes amiable
>   Hopes thee ; of flattering gales
>   Unmindfull. Hapless they
> To whom thou untry'd seem'st fair. Me in my vow'd
> Picture the sacred wall declares t' have hung
>   My dank and dropping weeds
>   To the stern God of Sea.

This is essential Milton, at once classic and classicist. The scrupulous, weighed and ordered, almost abstract

language, the severe rhythms, the clarity of outline and
faintness of colour are more Horatian, one might say,
than Horace himself.   Now turn to Fanshawe :

What Stripling now thee discomposes
In Woodbine Rooms, on Beds of Roses,
      For whom thy Auburn Haire
      Is spread, Unpainted Faire ?
How will he one day curse thy Oaths
And Heav'n that witness'd your Betroaths !
      How will the poor Cuckold,
      That deems thee perfect Gold,
Bearing no stamp but his, be mas'd
To see a suddain Tempest rais'd !
      He dreams not of the Windes
      And thinks all Gold that shines.
For me my Votive Table showes
That I have hung up my wet Clothes
      Upon the Temple Wall
      Of Sea's great Admirall.

It is worth note that both versions, with all their
studied compression, have about half as many words
again as the Latin (100 and 92 against 66) ; Conington's
has 104.   It may be remarked also that "showes that I
have hung up my wet Clothes" is an unimpeachably exact
translation of *me indicat uvida suspendisse vestimenta*.
There is no need to draw the moral.   But I will not dwell
either on the minor felicities of Fanshawe's rendering,
nor on its minor defects.   These last come under two
heads—slovenlinesses and quaintnesses.   Now the task
to which English poetry was setting itself in the latter
half of the seventeenth century was just this : to get
rid of slovenliness, and to get rid of quaintness.   Both
were in its blood, and the task was heavy, the labour
long.   The object was attained at last, but it was won at
a heavy price.   Milton stood apart from the movement,
in superb and haughty isolation.   His poetry, to put it

succinctly, has nothing to do with that of his contemporaries. Apart from him, the whole English poetry of his age, a mass of perplexing cross-currents among a vast number of minor poets, almost defies any attempt at classification. Organic growth or movement in it is difficult to trace. But later criticism instinctively and rightly fastened on Waller, a poet otherwise of but small account either for the quantity or the quality of his writing, as the clue to the labyrinth, the thread marking the central current. It is difficult now to understand how Waller got his great and long-continued reputation if we do not keep this in mind. He was smooth, Pope tells us, and we ask in some bewilderment what there is so very remarkable in being smooth. But this smoothness was just then the quality on which the whole efforts of literature in England were concentrating. In the critical essay at the end of Johnson's life of Waller, there is one casual phrase which is the key to the situation : " He seems," says Johnson, " always to do his best." To the new generation, the poetry of the Elizabethan and Jacobean age, with its exuberance, its daring unrestraint, had begun to seem an unweeded garden. " It cannot be denied," Johnson ends, after weighing Waller piece by piece and finding him light currency, " that he added something to our elegance of diction, and something to our propriety of thought." How important this end seemed may be judged from the amount of the sacrifice that was cheerfully made to reach it. By the time it was fully attained the jettison of poetry had been so great that in the eyes of a new reaction a century later it seemed there was nothing left worth saving : " Is Pope," people began to ask, " a poet at all ? " But what had been won was this, that English literature had been brought back into the main stream of European art and thought, and was prepared to take its place in the immense intellectual movement of the eighteenth century, the movement out of which rose the modern world.

The part which Fanshawe had in that large, strenuous task set before itself by the seventeenth century, the task of civilising letters and conquering the actual world for literature, was by no means inconsiderable. The work was done by him, as by many others both before and after him, mainly through assiduous translation. It was the century of translation in a different sense from either the preceding or the following one. In an earlier age, the classics, whether those of ancient Greece or Rome, or those of a more modern foreign civilisation, had been translated primarily for the sake of their contents, in order to give access to an otherwise unknown outer world. In them were the secrets of wisdom ; to have access to them was to possess the key of all knowledge. At a later period, the beginning of which cannot be definitely fixed, but which had definitely set in early in the eighteenth century, they came to be translated for the sake of trans-lation, as an exercise in style and in the practice of that secondary but far from useless or ignoble art which fills galleries with skilful copies of works by the great painters. This practice has lasted into our own day. Gradually, as happened in the sister art after the discovery of photo-graphy, these copies have been processed and multiplied ; they have reached an extraordinary level of technical fidelity, and give innocent pleasure to a thousand trans-lators and perhaps to several thousand readers. But in the intermediate period which we are now considering, the object and scope of translation were larger and its place in our literature was much more important. That period may roughly be said to begin with Harrington's *Ariosto* in 1591, and to end with Dryden's *Virgil* in

1697. It culminated early, in Fairfax's *Tasso* (1600) and Chapman's *Homer* (1610–1615), but it went on until the Restoration in unabated volume. Its object was to make the English language into a complete vehicle of poetical expression ; to make England into an organic member of the Republic of letters, and to fuse the life and progress of English poetry with those of the great world-movement outside of which it had hitherto stood.

In carrying out this great object, Fanshawe's work had, as we have seen, an important place. When the object was attained, his work, like that of his fellow-labourers in the same field, had served its purpose and gradually fell into oblivion. Only students of English literature can be expected to go back to it now, though both for its own sake and for its historical importance it deserves and repays study. Looked at from this point of view it all assumes coherence and correlation. His translations of Virgil and Horace, of Guarini, of Camoens, even of an author so wholly forgotten now as Antonio de Mendoza, were all attempts from different directions at extending the potentialities of English poetry up to the point that had been reached, at one time or another, by the poets of the two southern peninsulas. Even his Latin version of the *Faithful Shepherdess* represents another variation of the same impulse ; it was, in effect, the testing of Fletcher's pastoral play by a classical standard, and the vindication for it of a certain classical quality. Fanshawe states this object clearly in his own preface : " I do not see," he says—I give a paraphrase of his Latin—" that France or Spain or either ancient or modern Italy has any reason to slight the English Muses ; the harbours of England are open to foreign merchandise, and foreign harbours, at all events the free port of Latin, the world-language, need not be closed against English wares." In a beautiful little lyric, written in 1630, the year after Milton's *Ode on the Nativity*, Fanshawe had spoken of England as "a world without the world." The verses may well be quoted :

> Only the island which we sow
> (A world without the world) so far
> From present wounds, it cannot show
>   An ancient scar.
>
> White Peace, the beautifull'st of things,
> Seems here her everlasting rest
> To fix, and spreads her downy wings
>   Over the nest.
>
> As when great Jove's usurping reign
> From the plagu'd world did her exile,
> And tied her with a golden chain
>   To one blest isle :
>
> Which in a sea of plenty swam,
> And turtles sang on every bough :
> A safe retreat to all that came,
>   As ours is now.

What was being sown in England in these years was the dragon's teeth that came to harvest in the Civil Wars. But the commerce of literature, all through the disastrous times that followed, was making England, in a fuller sense than before, a world within the world of the mind.

No one can give more title in an estate than he himself possesses ; and the life of a translation, even otherwise transitory and precarious, is contingent on the life of its original. The reputation of both Guarini and Camoens is long ago faded ; it is difficult for us now to realise that the *Pastor Fido* had for a full century an almost unparalleled fame throughout Europe, and that the *Lusiads* were reckoned in the first rank of European epics, alongside of the *Gerusalemme Liberata*, and almost alongside of the *Iliad* and the *Aeneid*. They were translated into Italian, Spanish, French, and Latin, as well as into English. I cannot honestly recommend the reading of Fanshawe's *Lusiads* as a very enthralling occupation. There is a good deal of truth in the strictures passed on Fanshawe's version by Mickle in the preface to his own translation of 1775 :

bald, harsh, unpoetical . . . so obscure that the present translator has often been obliged to have recourse to the Portuguese to discover his meaning . . . in every page there are puns, conceits, and low quaint expressions, uncountenanced by the original.

But it remains interesting as a study of the development of English versification and the development of a vocabulary in English poetry. Of his *Pastor Fido* it is possible to speak in much higher terms. Guarini's famous pastoral play was meant to out-do the *Aminta*. It succeeded for the time in producing the desired effect. Tasso was said to have exclaimed after seeing it : " If he had not read my *Aminta*, he had not excelled it," just as he was said, according to an equally authentic tradition, to have confessed that he dreaded Camoens as a rival. But this sort of success can only be attained by forcing the note, and it cannot be permanent. Beside the limpid, soft beauty, the tender if somewhat effeminate grace of the *Aminta*, Guarini's work now seems a little coarse, a little common, more than a little mechanical. Yet it is impossible to deny its great ingenuity, melodiousness, and finish. Fanshawe's version reproduces these qualities very adequately except the last ; for English was not then on the whole, if it ever has been, so exquisitely finished a vehicle of poetry as Italian. The translation is full of lovely phrases and graceful passages.

These may be sought for rather than quoted ; I may just note in passing one half-line about the rose " cloistered up in leaves." It is certain as need be that Keats had never seen the volume ; but these, as will be remembered, are the exact words used by him in one of the two cardinal passages of *Endymion*.

The vitality of a translation, so far as it is a translation, is necessarily limited by the primary vitality of its original. But the converse proposition is not true ; for it is just those poems which possess, as nearly as anything human can, immortal life that perpetually demand retranslation. Virgil and Horace are among the immortals, the classics, not of one age or country, but of all time and all the world. Each age rediscovers and reinterprets them, and no translation can interpret more than one phase of their complex quality, their multiform significance. The attitude of any period towards poetry, the meaning that poetry has for any period, may be partly gauged by observing what it found in the classics, and what, therefore, it expressed in its translations. Thus Fanshawe's translations of the fourth book of the *Aeneid*, and of between forty and fifty of Horace's odes, are a sort of index, not only to his own scholarship, but to the kind of poetic appreciation which was then in the air and which was an actual directing force in the world of letters. I have already quoted his rendering of one of the Odes. Further instances, if they were multiplied, would only emphasise the quality we found there, the vivid sense of colour and of phrasing in the use of language, the swift insight into the thought of the original, and the subtle skill with which that thought is retranslated into new language ; and, alongside of all this, a certain pedestrian quality, an ease that verges on slovenliness, a certain failure in the noble simplicity, the reserve and precision

E

which are of the essence of classic work. Here are the
first, fourth, and fifth stanzas of the *Aequam memento* :

> Keep still an equal mind, not sunk
> With storms of adverse chance, not drunk
>   With sweet prosperity,
>   O Dellius that must die. . . .

> Bid hither wines and ointments bring
> And the too short sweets of the spring,
>   Whilst wealth and youth combine
>   And the Fates give thee line.

> Thou must forgo thy purchas'd seats
> Ev'n that which golden Tiber wets,
>   Thou must ; and a glad heir
>   Shall revel with thy care.

And here are stanzas 4–7 of the *Otium divos* :

> His little's much whose thrifty board
>   Shines with a salt that was his sire's ;
> Whose easy sleeps nor fears disturb
>   Nor vain desires.

> Why in short life eternal care ?
>   Why changing for another sun ?
> Who, having shunn'd his native air,
>   Himself could shun ?

> Take horse, rude Care will ride behind,
>   Embark, into thy ship she crowds,
> Fleeter than stags and the east wind
>   Chasing the clouds.

> Let minds of any joy possess'd
>   Sweeten with that whatever gall
> Is mix'd. No soul that e'er was blest
>   Was blest in all.

Nor can I deny myself the pleasure, or Fanshawe
himself the justice, of quoting a specimen of his translation of Virgil. It is needless to point in what respects,
or how much, it falls short of the magnificent original.

But it shows a gentleman's scholarship to perfection ; for combined dignity and sweetness it is, I think, unsurpassed by what any other rendering of Virgil into English has achieved.   The passage is from Dido's speech to her sister when sending her on a last despairing effort to turn Aeneas from his purpose.

> Yet try for me this once : for only thee
> That perjur'd soul adores, to thee will show
> His secret thoughts ; thou, when his seasons be,
> And where the man's accessible, dost know.
> Go, sister, meekly speak to the proud foe :
> I was not with the Greeks at Aulis sworn
> To raze the Trojan name, nor did I go
> 'Gainst Ilium with my fleet, neither have torn
> Anchises' ashes up from his profaned urn.
>
> Why is he deaf to my entreaties ? whither
> So fast ? it is a lover's last desire
> That he would but forsake me in fair weather
> And a safe time.   I do not now aspire
> To his broke wedlock-vow, neither require
> He should fair Latium and a sceptre leave.
> Poor time I beg, my passions to retire,
> Truce to my woe ; nor pardon, but reprieve,
> Till griefs, familiar grown, have taught me how to grieve.

There are traces still left here of the Elizabethan rhetoric, and of the post-Elizabethan mannerism ; but both are becoming subdued and civilised, while still possessing the glowing colour and melodious phrasing of that great school of poetry.   Just a little more, and Fanshawe would have attained what he and all his contemporaries were feeling after, the secret of a style which will never be obsolete.

Fanshawe's works have never been collected.   So far as I am aware, none of them, except in brief extracts, has ever been reprinted since a garbled version of his *Pastor Fido* was published, together with the

Italian, in 1726.   One could wish that this neglect were repaired.   I have, I hope, shown reason for rescuing them, both on their own account, and because of their value as documents illustrating the development of English poetry and poetical style.   The University of Cambridge surely owes some pious duty to the memory of one of her distinguished sons and one of her representatives in Parliament.   " He had the fortune," say the " Memoirs," " to be the first chosen and the first returned Member of the Commons House of Parliament in England after the King came home : and this cost him no more than a letter of thanks, and two braces of bucks, and twenty broad pieces of gold to buy them wine." The wine is long drunk, and Fanshawe long forgotten in Cambridge.   But the University of Milton and Dryden, of Gray and Wordsworth, of Byron and Tennyson owes a very special debt to poetry—and Fanshawe was not only a scholar and a statesman, but a poet.   On his monument in Ware Church, which is extant and in good preservation, among a long catalogue of the public offices which he filled, we read that he was *literarum luce praestantissimus.* The praise does not go beyond the exaggeration permissible in an epitaph, and the wording is happy ; for whether in the arduous task of public service or in the quiet happiness of home, literature, and in literature, poetry, was from first to last the light of his life.

POPE

The Leslie Stephen Lecture delivered before the University of Cambridge, 10 May 1919

POPE

WHEN I was honoured by the request to give a lecture on
this foundation, it seemed to me that I could not choose a
more appropriate subject than that great figure in English
letters on whom Leslie Stephen himself has written with
such mastery and insight. His monograph on Pope
appeared nearly forty years ago. It is a work admirable alike in its width and exactness of knowledge, in
its clarity, balance, and justice. As a critical biography
dealing with Pope's whole personality and his whole
historical and literary environment, it cannot be replaced,
and hardly even now requires to be supplemented. But
the revaluation and reinterpretation of an artist and his
art are another matter. On these there is no final judgment. Poetry means to each generation, even one might
say to each individual, something different. Its vital
quality varies with the temperament, the tradition, the
orientation of the minds which approach it. Hence all
poetry bears in itself the call for perpetual reinterpretation.

This is true of the steadiest poetical fames ; and that
of Pope has notoriously fluctuated, has been, almost from
his own time, the subject of acute controversy. To this
must be added, that appreciation or depreciation of his
poetry has been much deflected by irrelevant interests.
It has been treated far too often as ancillary to, or to be
judged by, his personal character on the one hand, and

the social, political, and intellectual life of his circle on the other. Mr. Courthope, for instance, bases its importance largely, or even mainly, on its personal interest and its historical value. But poetry as poetry is not a biographical or historical document. And criticism of his poetry has been much mixed up with the disparate problem of his own moral character. On this I do not propose to enlarge. It is a study of intense psychological interest, but not pleasant. Whatever record leaps to light under the searching analysis of his biographers only confirms the pitiless sentence of Macaulay, " lying and equivocation was the habit of his life " : of Leslie Stephen, " he was, if one must speak bluntly, a liar and a hypocrite " : of Mr. Courthope himself, " in the execution of his schemes there was no form of deceit, from equivocation to direct falsehood, which he hesitated to employ." But poetry is not to be so judged. Milton was not a shining example of the domestic virtues. Coleridge, it has been said, had no morals at all. When Pope writes :

Teach me to feel another's woe,
    To hide the fault I see ;
That mercy I to others show,
    That mercy show to me,

we may smile or sigh, or merely gasp ; but the question (as with the criticism made by Wordsworth's friends on his *Ode to Duty*) is not whether the poet observed his own precepts, but what is the quality of the poetry. In this as in so many other matters, the nineteenth century went widely astray. We must hark back and start afresh from a less confused view.

The customary belief as to Pope may be summed up thus : that, in virtue mainly of his later work, the *Essay on Man* and the *Satires* and *Epistles*, he occupied a place of unique and unchallenged supremacy in English poetry for fifty or sixty years ; that this tradition was broken towards the end of the century by the Romantic School ; that it finally died with Byron, so far as Byron's own estimate was not a provocative paradox ; and that attempts to reinstate it, then and since, have been artificial, like revivals of Queen Anne fashions in architecture or furniture. " Ever since the romantic movement of the early nineteenth century," Mr. Andrew Lang writes in his History of English Literature, " people have asked, Was Pope a poet ? " But both dates and facts of this customary belief are wrong. The Romantic revival itself began in Pope's own lifetime. Pope won his full fame by his early, and now generally decried or discredited, poetry. It was consolidated, rather than increased, by his Homer ; with his *Iliad*, completed by him at the age of thirty-two, it reached its climax. His later work, on which the greatest store is set by more recent critics, was received by its own generation rather with the respect due to the work of an acknowledged master than with the enthusiasm evoked by a substantive achievement. The *Essay on Man*, one might almost say, slunk into the world ; in 1738, Johnson's *London* halved the honours, if not more, with the *Epilogue to the Satires* ; and the definite reaction set in about a couple of years later. Pope had created a school and established a tradition. But neither the school nor the tradition was ever, except as regards technique of versification, dominant over the whole field of English poetry ; and even as regards that technique, Pope's rhymed couplet was never more than one among other established poetical forms ; both in and after his time, blank verse had quite an equal vogue. In the heroic couplet indeed, the type established by him had a dominating and cramping effect on his successors. Though in Johnson's hands it took an added weightiness, in Goldsmith's a new melodiousness, it remained for a long time substantially what Pope had made it, and it was not until the full disengagement of the Romantic movement that the tradition was broken. Cowper's saying that he

> Made poetry a mere mechanic art,
> And every warbler has his tune by heart,

is directed not against Pope himself, but against his imitators ; a similar criticism may be made on the post-Augustan Latin hexameter without any derogation from the praise of Virgil. Cowper's couplet immediately follows a high and just tribute to Pope's own " musical finesse " and " delicate touch." It was on matters of versification and diction, particularly the latter, that the attack of the Lake Poets was primarily based. On the more fundamental issue of his poetical quality they did not go beyond what had been openly said by critics half a century before.

When, or by whom, the daring question whether Pope were a poet was first raised, cannot perhaps be certainly determined. The famous sentence in the last paragraph of Johnson's Life is curiously, and it would seem purposely, uninforming as to this. " It is surely superfluous," he writes, " to answer the question that has once been asked, Whether Pope was a poet ? otherwise than by asking in return, If Pope be not a poet, where is poetry to be found ? " The allusion is generally read as referring to Joseph Warton's Essay published in 1756. But Warton, if he thought so, took care not to say so. Willing to wound, he was afraid, or felt himself unable, to strike. " I do not think him," he says, " at the head of his profession. What is there transcendently sublime or pathetic in Pope ? " The specific quality of

" the true poet " he defines as " a creative and glowing imagination " ; and this indeed he seems to deny to Pope, or to allow it only to a comparatively small portion of his work. Yet five and twenty years later, and in answer as may be conjectured to Johnson's Life of the year before, he insisted that it was a misinterpretation to make him insinuate that Pope was not a great poet, and that he only says, and thinks, that he was not the greatest. The fact is that the first counter-reaction in favour of Pope had then fully set in. A similar reaction has followed closely upon each successive wave of disparagement, and begun to take effect before that wave had reached its crest, so that, as in the resultant of two plotted curves, the level of his fame has rather undulated than swung sharply from elevation to depression. There is an interesting illustration of this prompt counter-reaction in that well-known chapter of " The Newcomes " where the Colonel listens in bewilderment to the literary talk of Clive and his friends. " He heard that there had been a wicked persecution against Mr. Pope's memory and fame, and that it was time to reinstate him " ; the plea of vindication was the first he had heard of the attack. The reference in this scene to the appearance of " the two volumes by young Mr. Tennyson of Cambridge " dates it : it was in the full movement of ascent, that is, of Wordsworthianism, and when the revulsion against the eighteenth century generally was just reaching its height.

Mr. Courthope, in the course of his own estimate of Pope's poetry, speaks of Leslie Stephen as too disparaging in his criticism, and as overborne by his Wordsworthian instincts. No doubt there is truth in this ; yet the fuller truth is that Stephen, while as a critic of thought, of morals, and of character, he was sound and penetrating, was without that touch of the poet in him which is necessary for the vital appreciation of poetry. He tends to regard poetry as if it were merely a variant of prose, to be weighed and judged on what might be called its prose value. Arnold himself was not wholly free from an analogous defect ; when he lays it down that " Dryden and Pope are not classics of our poetry, they are classics of our prose " he can hardly escape the alternative charge of wanton paradox or wilful confusion of the issue. Poetry is one thing, prose another. Clarity, precision, good sense are virtues in either. Pope has these, and in fact they are more conspicuous in his verse than in his prose. While Dryden is admittedly one of the great masters of English prose, Pope's, though it belongs to a good school, seldom reaches high excellence. Even at its best it is too elaborate and mannered and uneasy ; of his fine preface to the *Iliad* he said himself that it was " too much on the great horse." But it is not through these virtues in his poetry that Pope takes his rank as a poet.

Pope gave to his age, it has been said, the kind of poetry that it needed. This is true, and in no disparaging sense. But brilliant as was his success in doing so, one may trace in him from the first an unfulfilled promise, an aspiration beyond any actual accomplishment. Such a gift could not be hid. His contemporaries felt it, though they could not well understand it. It is only the existence of such a feeling which accounts for that amazing early conquest which swept him, in spite of every external disadvantage, to his supremacy. " A young poet, his name is Pope," Granville wrote when he first appeared on the horizon ; " he is not above seventeen or eighteen years of age, and promises miracles." When he was five and twenty, Swift called him the best poet in England. Nor was this a partial and merely insular judgment ; for Voltaire, a few years later, writes of " Mr. Pope, the best

poet of England, and at present of all the world." It
is not then astonishing, though it may lead us to revise
our point of view, that we find Warton, after Pope's
death, and when the first reaction against him was at its
height, deliberately expressing the opinion that " the
reputation of Pope as a poet among posterity will be
principally owing to his *Windsor Forest*, his *Rape of the
Lock*, and his *Eloisa to Abelard*."

To these now we would probably add the *Elegy*. It
is curious that Johnson, while he has nothing but praise
for the *Eloisa*, says of the *Elegy*, " Poetry has not often
been worse employed than in dignifying the amorous
fury of a raving girl."

The body of Pope's earlier poetry represented by these
pieces has since dwindled in its reputation. The *Pastorals*
by which he made his first fame are generally discredited
or ignored ; more so than a large judgment will fully
ratify. They suffer indeed from the mannerism of the
period ; but much of the condemnation bestowed on
them is really condemnation not of them, but of the
pastoral as a form of poetry. To that extent, it is vitiated
by the same failure of understanding, the incapacity to
appreciate poetry as art, which is at the root of Johnson's
attack on *Lycidas*. The charge of immaturity and conventionality may be, and is, made equally against Virgil's
Eclogues. Pope's *Pastorals* do not indeed like the
Eclogues mark the opening of a new age and a new birth
for poetry. But we may nevertheless find in them a
movement towards revolution, and the accents, still
unsustained and uncertain, of a new poetical voice.

> Where'er you walk, cool gales shall fan the glade,
> Trees, where you sit, shall crowd into a shade ;
> Where'er you tread the blushing flowers shall rise,
> And all things flourish where you turn your eyes—

these lines, so fine in phrasing, so elastic in rhythm, have become inseparable from the exquisite music to which Handel wedded them when he took the words for his opera of *Semele*. But their own faultless melodiousness melts into Handel's music like a tune into a tune. If we compare them with Pope's own extant first draft, we shall realise how from the first he was, what Warton denied, a great " inventor " (as we should now say, an imaginative creator) as well as a great improver. And from this we shall be led on to see, more largely, how, great as his achievement is, his aim and ambition were greater ; how they imply, and sometimes touch, those heights of poetry which are trodden by the immortals alone.

For such soaring flights of song the age indeed was not propitious ; though, if we look a little deeper, perhaps no age is. In our own poetry, Milton, Wordsworth, Tennyson, all make the same complaint of their age. Virgil had done so before them, and other poets, very likely, long before Virgil. A fine and true account of what Pope did for English poetry is given by himself in a piece where he is throughout at his best, the *Imitation of the Second Epistle of the Second Book of Horace*. What it needed, after the comparative anarchy of the previous century, was discipline. That requirement Pope met and fulfilled : but in a sense, he spent himself in doing so. The reaction against lawless romanticism, like all such reactions, overshot its mark ; it passed, even in Pope himself, and more disastrously in the school of those who had his tune by heart, down to the final degradation of Darwin and Hayley, into an academic and devitalised classicism. But Pope is more than a classicist ; he is an authentic classic, and in that sense in which the finest classical poetry includes and absorbs romance. And for Pope at his finest—by which

I mean, at his poetically highest—we have to go not to
the *Satires* and *Epistles*, but to the work of his early and
middle period ; oftener than is generally realised, to his
earlier poems.   In these there is, here and there, a beauty
of melody, a clear flame of imagination, such as seldom
recurs in his mature work.   That maturity was reached
through severe and cramping discipline, in a mind which
had fretted and laboured itself to exhaustion.   In these
too, the metrical mechanism, which afterwards became
unduly rigid, is still elastic and is already masterly.   In
one of his boyish trial-pieces, the translation from the
Thebaid, one comes on this :

> All birds and beasts lie hushed ; sleep steals away
> The wild desires of men and toils of day,
> And brings, descending thro' the silent air,
> A sweet forgetfulness of human care :

a little later, in the *Temple of Fame*, a piece which as a
whole is only an elaborate school-exercise, on this :

> How vain that second life in others' breath,
> The estate which wits inherit after death !
> Ease, health and life for this they must resign ;
> Unsure the tenure, but how vast the fine !

and between the two, in *Windsor Forest*, on the noble
passage—-too splendid to be insincere, one would say
without hesitation were it from the pen of any other poet
—on the life of the happy man, " wandering thoughtful
in the silent wood," the Muse and Nature his companions,
with its magnificent climax :

> Bids his free soul expatiate in the skies,
> Amid her kindred stars familiar roam,
> Survey the region, and confess her home.

To a poet who could write thus in youth, one might think
no height of Helicon was unscaleable.   But in Pope the

élan vital was from the first weak and intermittent. He was crippled by wretched health : " this long disease, my life," " that wretched state of health which God has been pleased to make my portion," of which he speaks so pathetically, was no over-description. He was the feeble child of old parents—his mother was forty-eight when he was born—sickly and almost if not quite deformed ; and over-study and over-excitation of the brain in his precocious childhood destroyed any chance there might have been of coaxing him into normal health. The frail machine was heavily over-engined ; and the body reacted on the mind. Hence his mixture of feverish ambition and morbid timidity, the self-consciousness which he could rarely shake off, the dissatisfaction with even his own best work that would never let him leave it alone, the fastidiousness which was not kept under control by either his pride or his good sense. At the age of twenty-seven, at the summit of his fame, not yet worn out by the ten years' labour of his Homer and the longer and more shattering war with the dunces, he writes that he is " out of humour with myself, fearful of some things, wearied of all." *Alas, the warped and broken board, how can it bear the painter's dye ?* Johnson notes, with true insight, that he was " a mind always imagining something greater than it knows, always endeavouring more than it can do." " What I wrote fastest," he said himself, " always pleased most." But his consciousness of his own genius never reached confidence in it ; he had not strength enough to stand alone, or to advance fearlessly in the realm that lay open to him. He fell under the domination of Swift ; he fell later, and as disastrously, under the domination of Bolingbroke ; he knew it, and stung back by treating both with inexcusable perfidy. He even crept under the shield of that gladiator with the soul of an attorney, the brazen-mouthed and iron-lunged Warburton. It was not from such sources that his own flame of creative imagination could be fed or rekindled. The genius which in a healthier and happier nature might have expanded magnificently, failing to find outlet, festered inwardly, became toxic, poisoned his life and infected his poetry. Even his pride—

Yes, I am proud, I must be proud to see
Men, not afraid of God, afraid of me—

was mixed up with pitiable cowardice. " Without courage," in the words of Scott, " there cannot be truth, and without truth there can be no other virtue." It is one of the tragic ironies of life that the great obstacle to Pope's fame is his own wretched anxiety for it. He could criticise himself, and does, with as much insight as any of his critics, but he could not liberate himself : "a bitter heart that bides its time and bites."

To this morbid self-consciousness it is due not only that he squandered his genius on petty personal rancours, not only that neither friend nor enemy, neither man nor woman, could ever safely trust him, but also that his work is often most superb where it fluctuates on the edge of burlesque. The *Rape of the Lock* is by general assent one of the few perfect things in English poetry. It is, in its kind, the high-water mark of poetry, and of no poetry in any kind can one say more. But further, it is worth remarking that what Johnson said of it, " New things are made familiar, and familiar things are made new," is the essential definition of poetry itself, and the note of poetry at its highest. It is in effect what Shelley says in one of his most profound and illuminating sentences : " Poetry lifts the veil from the hidden beauty of the world, and makes familiar objects be as if they were

F

not familiar." It was Pope's timidity and low vitality, not his good sense, that kept him moored to the ground. The *Essay on Man* is only the most conspicuous instance of what is characteristic of his work as a whole, that it has not full head of pressure behind it, that it falls short in large constructive power and in continuous inspiration.

This weakness was his, but it was likewise a weakness of his age. Pope's lifetime is almost coincident with a singular submergence of the lyrical instinct which before and after it has been the vitalising element in our poetry. It had kept it alive in the otherwise bleak and sterile century which followed Chaucer. It was the sap and life-blood of the Elizabethan age, when of every corner of the wide field of poetry it might be said,

Within this mile break forth a hundred springs.

In the seventeenth century it first spread into undisciplined luxuriance and then stagnated and was lost. In Dryden, as Gray observes in one of his fine criticisms, " the music of our old versification still sounded " : with him it disappeared. The so-called lyrical poetry of the first forty years of the eighteenth century is almost null, but for the group of hymn-writers, among whom, in virtue of two or at most three pieces which have taken a place beyond the reach of criticism, must be included Addison. Pope himself, in his *Universal Prayer*, just touched the fringe of the group. Except for this, his incursions into lyric poetry are wholly disastrous ; all that can be said in extenuation is that they are but few. The only one which is ambitious, his *St. Cecilia* ode, may fairly claim to be among the worst extant in an age conspicuous for badness. There is not a single good line in it. Thomas Warton was quite justified in saying that parts of it " have much the air of a drinking-song at a county election."

That submergence of the pure lyric meant the general enfeeblement of lyrical quality, of the singing voice, throughout the whole sphere of poetry. It did not indeed disappear ; if it had, poetry would have ceased : nor can it be justly said of it in Pope that the sound is forced, although the notes are few. It is authentically and nobly present in the *Elegy* ; still more so in the *Eloisa to Abelard*, which it fills throughout except for one unfortunate passage of ten lines and for the disastrous couplet which Pope, by some unaccountable hallucination, tacked on to the conclusion. It makes music in the *Rape of the Lock* ; it breaks out intermittently in the *Satires* and *Epistles*. It glitters fitfully, but often with extraordinary beauty, in the *Dunciad*.

> O born to see what none can see awake,
> Behold the wonders of the oblivious lake !

That may be called sublimated burlesque, without derogating from its rank as poetry. But there are many other passages as to which no question can be raised :

> Yet, yet a moment one dim ray of light
> Indulge, dread Chaos and eternal Night !

or, to come to the best at once, the incomparable

> Lo where Maeotis sleeps, and hardly flows
> The freezing Tanais through a waste of snows :

Pope's own favourite couplet, according to tradition, in the whole of his work. " The reason of this preference," Johnson observes, " I cannot discover." It was a pity he could not.

The admixture of pungent satire with high—all but the highest—authentic lyrical quality is perhaps most conspicuous in a justly famous passage in the *New Dunciad*. His theme is a savage attack on the fashionable

Grand Tour as part of the so-called education of the upper classes :

> Led by my hand, he sauntered Europe round,
> And gathered every vice on Christian ground.

But when he touches Italy his imagination, almost against his will, kindles into flame ; he speaks of her like an artist and a lover, " and when he speaks he seems to sing." All the magic of the South rises in his

> Love-whispering woods and lute-resounding waves.

With the exquisitely melodious and unforgettable phrases, " happy convents bosom'd deep in vines," and " lily-silvered vales," it is curious to compare those of Tennyson's *Daisy*, so like and yet so different ; the

> —high hill-convent, seen
> A light amid its olives green,

and the " milky-bell'd amaryllis " blowing on the beaches. The one is a landscape by Claude, the other a water-colour of the English school. Pope, like Tennyson, longed to travel ; and he longed to be a painter. He actually worked at painting under Jervas ; and all his allusions to the art are those of one who knows what he is talking about

The *Dunciad* as we possess it—for the earlier version has, I think, seldom been reprinted and is not much known except among students or specialists—is the last and the largest instance of that insatiable thirst for re-casting and remodelling his own work which pursued Pope like an obsession. Very often the remodelling did harm rather than good ; the triumphant success of the enlarged *Rape of the Lock* was achieved against a risk which Addison was quite right in deprecating, and Pope could not reasonably expect to repeat it. The concluding passage of the *New Dunciad* is poetry before which all criticism has bowed down in admiration. Spence mentions that Pope himself could not repeat it without his voice faltering. " And well it might," said Johnson when this was told him, " for they are noble lines." Thackeray was only summing up the consent of the generations when he wrote, " No poet's verse ever mounted higher than that wonderful flight. In these astonishing lines Pope reaches, I think, to the very greatest height which his sublime art has attained, and shows himself the equal of all poets of all times." The admiration can hardly be called excessive, or the praise extravagant. Yet appreciation may look closer and weigh in finer scales if we regard the passage in its germination and growth. We possess it in three successive forms. In the first edition of the original *Dunciad* it is only in germ and consists of but six lines :

> Then, when these signs declare the mighty year,
> When the dull stars roll round and reappear,
> Let there be darkness, the dread Power shall say ;
> All shall be darkness, as it ne'er were day ;
> To their first chaos wit's vain works shall fall
> And universal darkness cover all.

The thought is there ; and in this first sketch there are already two of the immortal phrases. But the art has not wrought itself out : the expression halts, and the fourth line is quite feeble and vapid. In the revised edition of the next year, the six lines have become twenty-two, and have been transfigured. When he remodelled the whole poem a dozen years later, Pope took out the magnificent opening couplet, and reinserted it with some alteration, rather awkwardly, a little further back in Book III ; the remaining twenty lines he completely rewrote and expanded into thirty. Five couplets are added ; the order

of the others is materially changed, and only four are left
unaltered in wording. Preference here is a matter of
opinion ; I can only express my own, and quote the
whole passage in what I hold to be its noblest and most
perfect form :

> Signs following signs lead on the mighty year ;
> See ! the dull stars roll round and reappear.
> She comes ! the cloud-compelling Power, behold !
> With Night primeval, and with Chaos old.
> Lo ! the great Anarch's ancient reign restored ;
> Light dies before her uncreating word.
> As one by one, at dread Medea's strain,
> The sickening stars fade off the ethereal plain ;
> As Argus' eyes, by Hermes' wand oppressed,
> Closed one by one to everlasting rest ;
> Thus at her felt approach and secret might
> Art after art goes out, and all is night.
> See skulking Truth in her old cavern lie,
> Secured by mountains of heaped casuistry :
> Philosophy, that touched the heavens before,
> Shrinks to her hidden cause, and is no more :
> See Physic beg the Stagyrite's defence !
> See Metaphysic call for aid on sense !
> See mystery to Mathematics fly !
> In vain ! they gaze, turn giddy, rave, and die.
> Thy hand, great Dulness ! lets the curtain fall,
> And universal darkness buries all.

The first reaction against Pope did not touch his
Homer. The only disparaging criticism made on it for
half a century was Bentley's on its first appearance, if we
neglect, as we may, the attacks of the dunces. Bentley's
comment stung Pope, as all criticism did ; but it was too
obviously true, and too free from anything like malice,
to sting even him deeply. He nursed his tepid resent-
ment for twenty years, according to his habit, but his
rejoinder, the portrait of Aristarchus in the *New Dunciad*,
brought out with a characteristic mixture of caution and

malice when Bentley was dying, is not venomous, it is (for Pope) almost good-natured. Bentley's criticism was that of a scholar ; the opinion of the world at large was that expressed by Johnson, " it is the greatest work of the kind that has ever been produced." This judgment he deliberately reaffirmed when in the Life of Pope he wrote, " It is certainly the noblest version of poetry which the world has ever seen . . . that poetical wonder . . . a performance which no age or nation can pretend to equal." Here Gray and Johnson, for once in their lives, were in agreement. " There would never," Gray had said even more emphatically, " be another translation of the same poem equal to it." His prophecy has so far been justified, at least as concerns the *Iliad*, which is what he spoke of, and what is usually meant when Pope's Homer is spoken of. No translation of any great work of art can in the nature of things be final ; still less can it replace the original ; but Pope's *Iliad* remains an English classic. If it were read more now, it would be depreciated less. For seventy years it held the field un-challenged. Since then the task has been reattempted by dozens of hands, from Cowper's to those of the present day ; it will be resumed, no doubt, by each age so long as the *Iliad* and the English language survive. Many of these translations have been skilful and competent ; most of their authors have, it is needless to say, approached their task with a far better equipment of scholarship than Pope. But none of their versions has lived, and Pope's does.

The Augustan diction was established by Pope's *Iliad* more than by any other work ; it was by it that, in the famous phrase, he " tuned the English tongue." Its defects are matter of common knowledge, into which it is needless to enter. When it became a fettering tradition,

it provoked a violent revolt. After the liberation had
been fully effected, it took its proper place in history,
and its merits as well as its defects can be more justly
appreciated. These merits are lucidity and dignity. In
reading Pope's Homer one can never be at a moment's
loss for the meaning ; and his power, in his chosen
medium, of rising to the occasion, of kindling to the
heroic temper and giving the Homeric thrill, is unequalled
and, one may dare to say, unsurpassable. "Triviality
and meanness"—the words are not those of a con-
servative reactionary, but of Wordsworth in the Preface
to the *Lyrical Ballads*—are " a defect more dishonourable
than false refinement." With Wordsworth's further
contention that this defect is " less pernicious in the sum
of its consequences " we are not here concerned ; Pope
was not responsible for the sum of the consequences of
his art, but for his art itself. But to raise the issue of
artificiality cuts both ways. In the time, now well over,
when the *Iliad* and *Odyssey* were thought of as " natural "
opposed to " artificial " epics, the Augustan diction stood
necessarily condemned. We know now that they are
not natural growths of untrained genius, but the consum-
mation of an extraordinarily elaborate art ; an art as
elaborate and as artificial, as conventional in the full
sense, as Pope's own. Those very phrases of " pseudo-
poetic diction " as it was called, which a century ago
goaded the romanticists into fury—the " conscious
swains " or the " fleecy care "—having lost their domination, have lost their power to annoy. They are one kind
of literary diction, like any other. The Biblical vocabulary
which Butcher and Lang's *Odyssey* brought into vogue
forty years ago—*waxeth faint, gat him up, howbeit* and *yea
now* and *verily*—has already become faded and obsolete.
Pope's diction was of its age, was living ; the other was

only an archaistic revival whose joints were rather
marrowless and blood decidedly cold. The Augustan
diction is that of a long past age, but the blood still pulses
in it. In Pope's rendering of the parting of Hector and
Andromache, to take one notable instance, there are about
two hundred continuous lines without a single inadequate
phrase, a single flat or jarring note, even after two hundred
years. " You must not call it Homer " : but it is Homer
magnificently reincarnated.

Even here, Pope was hampered by his own timidity.
From the extant fragments of his rough drafts one can
see how he often shrank from what his poetical instinct
had shown him ; how in his anxiety to forestall the charge
of being what was called " low " he became mannered,
and in his sensitiveness to an accusation of " incorrect-
ness " became monotonous ; how he would keep polish-
ing his verse until it lost its ripple and edge.

The simile at the end of the eighth *Iliad* has been
habitually cited to prove both his artificiality and his
insensitiveness to nature. As it left his hands finally it
cannot be defended ; it is in his worst manner ; the
images are blurred away, the diction is unnatural. If we
turn to his first hand, we can reconstruct from it a rendering which, though not faultless, must be freed of the
heavier censure.

> As when the moon in all her lustre bright
> O'er heaven's pure azure sheds her silver light,
> When no loose gale disturbs the deep serene,
> And not a cloud o'ercasts the solemn scene ;
> Around her throne the vivid planets glow,
> And stars unnumbered trembling beams bestow.
> O'er the dark trees clear gleams of light are shed
> And tip with silver every mountain head ;
> The valleys open, and the forests rise :
> All nature stands revealed before our eyes.

The failure here is not in realisation or in diction ; it is in the monotony of the metrical construction. The heroic couplet as regularised by Pope has undeniably this fault. He overdid his work on it ; and the larger, freer movement of which in the hands of a few masters before and after him it has proved capable, if it was within his compass, was not consistent with his method of distillation and concentration. His couplets stand apart from one another, like beads on a string ; and within the couplet, there is an increasingly uniform metrical balance both between the two lines of the couplet and the two halves of the line. In three of these five couplets the second line begins with " and " ; Pope is becoming a victim to the see-saw movement which his own ear felt and which he expressly condemns. This defect is worst where he has spent the most pains ; there are six of these " and " lines in the eleven couplets of the wonderful Atticus passage. In the *Epilogue to the Satires*, it has been noted, there is a reversion to a freer pattern ; but by that time the mischief was done. Pope had concentrated wholly on this single form of verse, and he became enmeshed in it. The result is that he comes not only to write but almost to think in couplets, and sometimes justifies Coleridge's impatient complaint that "the mechanical metre determines the sense." "A style too pointed and ambitious, and a versification too timidly balanced," Wordsworth observes more temperately and more justly.

It is the less surprising then that in the *Odyssey*, a task undertaken without enthusiasm and carried out with less than his usual meticulous care, he frees himself more from this cramping regularity. His portions of the *Odyssey* are the work of a tired man—" and Homer, damn him, calls "—and often the work is scamped, mechanical, no better than that of his two ghosts, and in fact indistinguishable from theirs, or at least from Fenton's. Where it is bad, it justifies the worst strictures made on it.

Her beauteous cheeks the blush of Venus wear,
Chastened with coy Diana's pensive air :

pseudo-poetic diction could hardly go beyond that as representing the pellucid line " like Artemis or golden Aphrodite." But where it is good, it is his workmanship at its best, for he has not spoiled it by over-anxiety. Take his very first lines, the opening of Book III (Books I and II were left by him to his assistants) :

The sacred sun, above the waters raised,
Through Heaven's eternal brazen portals blazed,
And wide o'er earth diffused his cheering ray
To gods and men to give the golden day.

But for the over-use of epithet—the besetting sin, as Goldsmith noted in one of his moments of singular insight, of the whole Augustan and post-Augustan age in English poetry—this is admirable. It may, however, be remarked in passing as a good instance of a peculiarity of Pope's couplet which has not, so far as I am aware, been ever noticed ; his propensity to rhyming on the $\bar{a}$ vowel sound. Probably he was unconscious of it himself. From his earliest work to his latest, one constantly comes on six or eight consecutive lines of it ; and I have noted, in his translation from the *Thebaid*, an instance, which may not be unique, where if a single couplet were removed, this assonance would run on for twenty.

Or again in Book V, the whole speech of Calypso to Ulysses and his reply are quite admirable, and may be set almost beside Pope's matchless rendering of the parting of Hector and Andromache in the *Iliad*. In this same Book,

> Let kings no more with gentle mercy sway
> Or bless a people willing to obey,
> But crush the nations with an iron rod,
> And every monarch be the scourge of God ;

or in Book XIV,

> From God's own hand descend our joys and woes ;
> These he decrees, and he but suffers those :
> All power is his, and whatsoe'er he wills
> The will itself, omnipotent, fulfils ;

the thought is modernised, as in a modern translation which purports to be more than a mere mechanical rendering it must be, and in some sense even ought to be ; and in the latter of the two passages, Pope has, as he often does, completely misunderstood his Greek (τὸ μὲν δώσει, τὸ δ' ἐάσει) from sheer defect of scholarship. Yet of such passages one may again say that if you must not call them Homer, they are nevertheless nobly Homeric.

Whether Pope might have avoided the stiffening and partial sterilisation of the rhymed couplet if he had practised it less exclusively would be a curious rather than a profitable enquiry. It was probably from some feeling of discontent with its limits (or rather, with his own self-created limits in handling it) that towards the end of his life he attempted, apparently for the first time, to write in blank verse. Of his unfinished epic of Brutus no remnant survives. " Part of the MS., in blank verse, now lies before me," Ruffhead writes in his Life (1769) ; but most annoyingly he omits to give even a single specimen. We could have spared for that the detailed prose sketch of its contents, which Ruffhead prints in full ; what matters is not the story, but the treatment. Would Pope's blank verse have been (as is not improbable) like that of Young, as Young's couplet-verse is like Pope's ? Would it have turned out little more than rhymeless couplets ? or might he perhaps have found in the new medium an access of fresh inspiration ? But the epic, like his other unfulfilled project of " an ode or moral poem on the folly of ambition," placed in the mouth of a shepherd among the ruins of Blenheim, is a vanished ghost.

It may sound a paradox ; but the fact is that Pope's poetry—the same remark applies to others among our great English poets—was not quite in the full central line of evolution. He did miracles, as had been prophesied of him ; but his young promise was not wholly fulfilled. He became cramped, not merely by classicism, but by an artificially limited scope of interest ; and, of course, matter reacted on style. He was a lonely genius, without the powerful vitality which can draw sustenance from the whole of what life has to offer, and without the ice-brook's temper which is necessary for genius if it is to live and thrive alone. Of all the contemporaries who influenced him it may be said that they only did him harm as a poet. Most of all is this true of Swift, the older and stronger man who dominated over Pope's weaknesses and stimulated his faults. The " unnatural delight in ideas physically impure " was unhappily common to both ; and common to both was an attitude towards women which is to many minds hardly less disgusting. " Most women have no characters at all " may have been, as Pope says it was, Martha Blount's saying and not his own. At all events he seized it and wallowed in it. His cynicism with regard to women is really

sentimentality gone tainted ; some would say, gone
putrid.   In his

> Matter too soft a lasting mark to bear
> And best distinguished by black, brown, or fair,

we have travelled a long way from the seventeenth century
light-heartedness ; from Suckling's gay couplet,

> The black, the brown, the fair shall be
> But objects of variety.

But still more remarkable is the contrast it presents to
the note of modern romanticism :

> C'est chose bien commune
> De soupirer pour une
> Blonde, châtaine, ou brune
>   Maîtresse,
> Lorsque brune, châtaine
> Ou blonde, on l'a sans peine—

so far following Pope almost verbally ; and then,

> Moi, j'aime la lointaine
>   Princesse.

This, it may be said, is modern sentimentality.   The
Augustan age too was sentimental, in its fashion.   But
it drank its sentiment out of a different jug.

Pope is the fullest of all English poets, Shakespeare
only excepted, of " quotations "—lines or phrases which
have become part of our common speech and incorporated in the structure of our common thought.   This
is itself high praise ; but it is not the praise of poetry,
which is a subtler thing.   The whole of *Paradise Lost*
has contributed only some half-dozen such.   Young, a
poet only of the second or third rank and now almost forgotten, comes I think next after Pope in their abundance.
But it is perhaps to these in the first instance that Pope

owes his widest and most continuous popular appreciation ; and in the second instance, to his " characters " ; to those highly wrought, incisive, elaborately polished passages, detachable from their context, in which he has etched with his mordant acid, and left as imperishable portraits, the souls of men and women whom he loved or hated. Chiefly, they are of those whom he hated ; the most brilliant are the most venomous, of those whom he hated, having once loved or admired. His own attempt at excuse—

Then why so few commended ?—Not so fierce ;
Find you the virtue, and I'll find the verse—

is too cynical to carry any conviction. His love was febrile and sickly ; his hatred was a clear consuming flame.

I remember, some five and thirty years ago, spending an evening with Mr. Courthope and Mr. Lang, when they fought over the old debate as to Pope's poetical quality, and left it a drawn battle. Mr. Courthope's view has been fully and repeatedly set forth by himself, in his Life of Pope, in his Oxford lectures, and again in his " History of English Poetry." It was unaltered throughout his life. Mr. Lang then—he modified his opinion later, more in his friendly antagonist's direction— would only admit that Pope's work was " poetry with a difference." Well, all poetry is poetry with a difference ; and it is going the wrong way about to object to one kind of poetry because it is not another kind. If Pope is thought of as a satirist, satire is to be sure not poetry at its highest, is not poetry doing all it can ; though even so it is doing what nothing but poetry can do, and one may remember that Dante places Horace, not the Horace of the Odes, but the Horace of the Satires, *Orazio satiro*, among the five great poets.   But Pope was much more than a satirist.

It is recorded of him that he liked Tasso better than Ariosto ; and the eighteenth century comment on the fact is significant ; " his taste had not been vitiated, like Milton's, by much reading of the Gothic romances of chivalry."   It is not usual to think of Milton as a lyrist and a romanticist ; but essentially he was both, and unless he had been, he could not have come to be, in the full and complete sense of the word, a classic.   Pope is a limited classic, a classic with a difference.   But with that difference, within that limit, his poetry is, as only classics are, imperishable.   No lapse of time, no change of fashion, can abate " that brilliant genius and immense fame."

THE POET OF THE SEASONS

An Address given to the Twickenham Literary and Scientific Society, 6 December 1920

THE POET OF THE SEASONS

THE place of Thomson among the English poets, the
quality of his poetry, and his great historical influence,
are matters on which the last word has yet to be said, and
which both require and repay consideration. This no
doubt applies in some degree to all poets ; but very
specially to those of that great germinal age, the eighteenth
century, which we are only now beginning to get into
perspective and to appreciate. The material for such
appreciation has in recent years been greatly augmented ;
and, as regards Thomson in particular, by two works of the
first importance. The one is Mr. J. Logie Robertson's
critical edition, in which for the first time a fully discrimi-
nated text has been supplied of a poem, or body of poetry,
which for twenty years was subjected by its author to incessant revision, and " underwent," in Mr. Robertson's
words, " changes of every conceivable kind. As long as he
lived and had the leisure (he never wanted the inclination)
he was revising and altering. He added and he modified,
withdrew and restored, condensed and expanded, substi-
tuted and inverted, distributed and transferred." The
other is the able and exhaustive study, *James Thomson : Sa
Vie et ses Œuvres*, by M. Léon Morel, one of that brilliant
company of French scholars, of whom M. Legouis is the
recognised head, who have earned our admiration and
gratitude by their masterly work on English literature.

The popularity and the fame of Thomson were for nearly a century unbounded in his own country, and very great beyond it. Not less important than his effect on the public was his influence on the poets and on the course of poetry during that period.

It was by *The Seasons* that both his fame and his influence were established ; and " the Poet of the Seasons " came to be the current synonym for his name. But his other work must be taken into account in order to form any fair estimate of his poetical quality. A good deal of it is juvenile or minor or occasional verse which does not count for much one way or another. His tragedies, *Sophonisba*, *Agamemnon*, *Edward and Eleanora*, *Tancred and Sigismunda*, *Coriolanus*, are as dead as the ill-starred efforts, in this kind of poetry, of all his contemporaries. Like those others, they were written partly for fashion, but very largely for profit. That was double ; for not only did the representation of a tragedy at Drury Lane or Covent Garden bring in a substantial sum to the author if it were not a total first-night failure, but the sale for tragedies printed after actual production was ordinarily larger than than that for other poetry. Johnson received £100 for *Irene*, and only £15 for *The Vanity of Human Wishes*. Two of Thomson's five tragedies had a distinct success. His first, *Sophonisba*, was produced at Drury Lane on February 28, 1730. It had what was then considered the long run of ten nights ; and the result was that four editions of it were called for within the year. All of it that effectively survives is the famous line :

O Sophonisba, Sophonisba, O !

But the popular story of the reception of this line on the first night and its hasty alteration has unfortunately to be dismissed as legendary. In all the editions of 1730, and even in the collected edition of 1738, the original line remains, and the alteration into

O Sophonisba, I am wholly thine,

was only made later. It is true, however, that it created some amusement at the time ; for it was parodied at once by Fielding in his brilliant *Life and Death of Tom Thumb the Great.* The *Agamemnon* of 1738 had only a fair success on the stage, but even so ran into two editions ; that of the *Tancred and Sigismunda,* seven years later, was again quite great. Of the other two, *Edward and Eleanora* was refused licence on political grounds ; *Coriolanus* was only finished a little time before the author's death. But meanwhile the revolution from the drama to the novel, both for tragic and for comic purposes, had been decisively made. The English tragic drama had been continuous, and continuously vital, from Marlowe to Otway ; then it sickened and died. With the publication in 1740 of *Pamela,* " le roman," in the striking and just words of M. Morel, " mit fin à la longue agonie de la tragédie en la tuant. Il la remplaçait par la forme d'art la plus souple, la plus plastique, la plus propre à se transformer selon les variations du goût, des milieux, et des temps."

But much later than this, it is amusing and not uninstructive to read the opinion of John Wesley (who had never a moment's doubt of his own competence both as a poet and a critic of poetry) on Thomson's tragedies. In his Journal, October 14, 1762, he notes :

A book was given me to write on, the works of Mr. Thomson, of whose poetical abilities I had always had a very low opinion ; but looking into one of his tragedies, *Edward and Eleanora,* I was agreeably surprised. The sentiments are just and noble, the diction strong, smooth and elegant; and the plot conducted with the utmost art, and brought off in a most surprising manner.   It is quite his masterpiece.

Of lyrical poetry Thomson wrote little.   But the *Hymn on Solitude* (printed in 1729) is of great beauty; it anticipates the pure line and liquid cadence of Collins. The *Nuptial Song*, of less excellence, is noteworthy as having been plundered by that sweet thief, Gray.   The lines

> The feathered lovers tune their throat,

and

> For long the furious God of War
> Has crushed us with his iron car,

sound curiously familiar ; because they recur so nearly in the *Ode on Spring*,

> The Attic warbler pours his throat,

and in the *Progress of Poesy*,

> On Thracia's hill the Lord of War
> Has curbed the fury of his car.

What Gray stole or borrowed, he knew of course how to make his own.   So too, however, to a large extent, did Thomson himself, who was a careful student and a skilful copyist of his own poetical predecessors, and whose thefts or borrowings are often very felicitous.

And once more, his little known lines *To the God of Fond Desire* have a combination of melodiousness and precision that makes them, in their kind, perfect.   They deserve quotation.

> One day the God of fond desire
>   On mischief bent, to Damon said,
> Why not disclose your tender fire,
>   Not own it to the lovely maid ?

The shepherd marked his treacherous art,
   And softly sighing thus replied,
'Tis true, you have subdued my heart,
   But shall not triumph o'er my pride.

The slave in private only bears
   Your bondage, who his love conceals,
But when his passion he declares,
   You drag him at your chariot-wheels.

As a lyric poet however, though not negligible, he is inconspicuous. Yet curiously, it is by a single couplet in a single and not otherwise remarkable lyric that he became part of the common consciousness of the whole nation ; and more curiously still, this couplet, which has been on all men's lips for nearly two hundred years, is seldom associated with his name, and even his authorship of it has been questioned, and cannot be said to be demonstrably certain.

On August 1, 1740, a fête was given by Frederick, Prince of Wales, at Clifden. For it, a masque on the subject of King Alfred was commanded ; the music for it was written by Arne, and the libretto was produced in collaboration by Thomson and Mallet, his friend, contemporary, and compatriot, who then held a salaried post in the Prince's household. One of the songs in it became, at once and by common spontaneous instinct, the national anthem. The chorus ending each of its six stanzas ran :

Rule, Britannia, rule the waves ;
Britons never will be slaves.

Misquoted as they usually (like so many famous phrases) are, the words have, from then until now, been known, it may be said, by every man, woman and child in England. Such universal and prolonged currency is, to be sure, no hall-mark of high poetry ; yet few of our poets can put such a feather in their cap.

For the authorship of this couplet there is no direct and unimpeachable evidence. Mallet was in some respects a feebler Thomson, and wrote very like him. The particular song in question may have been a joint product. But on a review of the internal evidence and of the arguments that have been brought forward on both sides, there seems sufficient reason to assign the song to Thomson's pen.

It is quite possible that he would have wished to rest his highest claim on what was his greatest failure, the dreary and all but unreadable *Liberty*. It is said that he thought it his best work ; and his letters show his deep mortification at its falling dead. He even eagerly lapped up Aaron Hill's coarse flattery : " an inimitable master-piece " ; " an immortal pyramid " ; equalling or excelling " whatever School-enthusiasm has misdreamt of Homer." It consists of between three and four thousand lines of blank verse, in the mixture of history, philosophy, politics and preaching on which poets always make shipwreck when they fail to fuse disparate and impracticable material by the heat of poetical genius. It occupied him for several years after the completion of *The Seasons*, and was brought out in five successive parts between 1734 and 1736. It was still-born ; and it should not be forgotten, for Thomson's credit, that when it proved a complete failure he voluntarily cancelled the agreement he had made for it with Millar the publisher. The best that can be said of it is that it has a few touches of description or sentiment which would not be unworthy of a place in *The Seasons*. Otherwise it is both tumid and empty ; flatter than the flattest parts of *The Excursion*, and as pedestrian, notwithstanding its heightened and even pompous diction, as the weakest pages of *The Task*.

If *Liberty* is an ambitious failure, Thomson's last

published poem, *The Castle of Indolence*, is the one in
which his poetical genius reaches its highest point.
There is indeed hardly any other poem which presents in
so small a compass—it is less than 1500 lines in all—so
strange a mixture of lovely romance and commonplace
burlesque.   It was taken up by him at intervals over a
dozen years at least, in the course of which it became a
sort of rag-bag, towards the contents of which both
Armstrong and Lyttelton contributed.   The whole of the
second canto is in fact valueless ; it trails on anyhow,
until the key has dropped from that of *The Eve of
St. Agnes* to that of *The Cap and Bells.* But the
earlier portion of the poem would be hard to surpass for
imaginative vision and melodiousness ; in its period, it
is unapproached.   For the first time in the eighteenth
century, the romantic note is struck fully and with certainty.   He was, whether he knew it or not, in advance
of his age ; partly from indolence, partly perhaps from
timidity, he did not pursue the splendid path on which he
had entered.   Wordsworth's praise of the imaginative
genius of *The Castle of Indolence*, in his Supplemen-
tary Preface of 1815, is well known, and is just.   But it
has remained true what Wordsworth then added : " that
fine poem was neglected on its appearance, and is at this
day the delight only of a few."   Even Gray failed to
appreciate it : he writes to Mason, " There is a poem lately
published by Thomson, called *The Castle of Indolence*,
with some good rhymes in it."   It opens as a frank
imitation of Spenser ; yet of the copy, if we choose to
call it so may be said, what can be said of very few copies,
that it recaptures the music, and revives the beauty, of
its original.   The greater part of the first canto, while
still drenched in Spenserianism, is substantive and wholly
original poetry.   Neither in the sixteenth nor in the

nineteenth century has this form of verse ever been used
with greater skill and beauty. The poets who have written
in it have perforce imitated Spenser ; he invented the
stanza and impressed his own genius on it imperishably.
But neither Byron nor Keats nor Shelley, nor those
others who, like Wordsworth and Tennyson, have just
touched it, have drawn from it a sweeter or more subtly
modulated music than Thomson does in passages where
he discards all tinge of parody and soars beyond merely
imitative romanticism :

> Was naught around but images of rest,
> Sleep-soothing groves and quiet lawns between :
>
> Join'd to the prattle of the purling rills
> Were heard the lowing herds along the vale,
> And flocks loud-bleating from the distant hills,
> And vacant shepherds piping in the dale :
>
> A pleasing land of drowsihead it was,
> Of dreams that wave before the half-shut eye
> And of gay castles in the clouds that pass
> For ever flushing round a summer sky :

or the miraculous stanza, almost too familiar to quote, but
which yet must needs be quoted :

> As when a shepherd of the Hebrid isles
> Placed far amid the melancholy main,
> Whether it be lone fancy him beguiles,
> Or that aerial beings sometimes deign
> To stand embodied to our senses plain,
> Sees on the naked hill or valley low
> The whilst in ocean Phoebus dips his wain
> A vast assembly moving to and fro ;
> Then all at once in air dissolves the wondrous show.

Twenty years before the date usually assigned for the
origins of the romantic movement, sixty before its full
flower, we have its note here in the fullest, amplest, most
authentic tone. So much must be noted with regard to

Thomson's poetical work before going on to a study of *The Seasons*, on which, as I said, and in effect on which alone, he made his fame, imposed his taste, and secured his public.

Thomson created descriptive poetry ; or if this be thought too sweeping a statement, he established it as a substantive poetic type ; and that not for Great Britain only, but for Europe. Pope, according to the saying of his recorded by Warton, thought descriptive poetry " as absurd as a feast made up of sauces." In the *Prologue to the Satires* he writes of his own early poetry,

> Soft were my numbers ; who could take offence
> While pure description held the place of sense ?

and in this he expressed a common opinion. Thomson, with the publication of *Winter*, launched a poetic revolution. His own immediate inspiration was, as he himself tells us, a poem entitled *A Winter's Day*, by Robert Riccaltoun (1691-1769)—now a forgotten name—which appeared in Savage's *Miscellany* for 1726, but was probably known to Thomson in MS. earlier. In that same volume of the *Miscellany* was also printed Dyer's *Grongar Hill*, an irregular ode which is a significant landmark in the movement towards naturalism. These had followed on Ramsay's *Gentle Shepherd* of 1725. *Winter*, *Summer*, and *Spring* were successively published, in that order, early in the years 1726, 1727, and 1728 ; *The Seasons* as a whole, with the inclusion of *Autumn*, in June 1730. Pope had then completed his Homer and published his first *Dunciad;* the *Essay on Man* and the great *Epistles* were yet to come. These dates give a new idea of the variety and volume of poetical movement in what is often thought of as a period of sterile classicism.

The success of Thomson's adventure was almost immediate. A year before, he had come to London from

Scotland, young, poor and unknown. *Winter* is said indeed to have hung fire just at first, when it was published, as a thin sixteen-page folio costing a shilling, in March. " It lay neglected," says Warton, " till Mr. Spence made honourable mention of it in his Essay on the *Odyssey;* which, becoming a popular book, made the poem universally known." This is quite untrue. Spence's Essay as published three months after *Winter* contains no reference, direct or indirect, to Thomson ; and *Winter* had before then gone into a second edition ; two more were called for before the end of the year. Its success has similarly, and probably with as little foundation, been attributed to Mitchell, afterwards an ambassador at Berlin, to Rundle (Pope's Rundle, who had become Bishop of Derry when he was immortalised by half a line in the *Epilogue to the Satires*), and to others. The successive parts were received with a growing chorus of admiring appreciation. They did not come into competition with the work of any contemporary, and roused no jealousies ; and in any case, Thomson's easy good-nature was irresistible. Pope not merely subscribed to the sumptuous first edition of the complete *Seasons* ; he helped largely, with advice and suggestion, in the minute revision through which the poem repeatedly went for subsequent editions. The copy of the edition of 1738, with marginal alterations and insertions in Pope's hand, is now in the British Museum. Some of the most beautiful passages as they now stand are in effect Pope's rather than Thomson's work. It will be sufficient to cite one instance. Lines 207–217 of *Autumn* now stand thus :

> Thoughtless of beauty, she was beauty's self,
> Recluse amid the close-embowering woods.
> As in the hollow breast of Apennine
> Beneath the shelter of encircling hills

A myrtle rises far from human eye,
And breathes its balmy fragrance o'er the wild,
So flourished blooming and unseen by all
The sweet Lavinia ; till at length, compelled
By strong necessity's supreme command,
With smiling patience in her looks she went
To glean Palemon's fields.

As it stood originally the passage ran :

Thoughtless of beauty, she was beauty's self
Recluse among the woods ; if city dames
Will deign their faith. And thus she went, compelled
By strong necessity, with as serene
And pleased a look as patience can put on,
To glean Palemon's fields.

The expansion and insertion are Pope's work. A detailed comparison of the successive versions may be commended to students of English literature in the eighteenth century ; it is instructive and full of interest. The edition of 1744 may be taken for this purpose as the definite form which the poem assumed, though a few slight alterations were made even later. There are over a thousand lines more in it than there were in the first collected edition of 1730 (5413 against 4349, exclusive of the Hymn). In the successive additions it is to be noticed that Thomson concedes more and more to the prevalent taste of the time by the insertion of philosophical or historical passages and the introduction of substantive episodes.

There are three of these narrative episodes in the whole poem. All three are perhaps mistakes. They give the feeling of being insertions or accretions, superfluous to the scheme of the work, and a little out of tone in their handling. The idyl of Palemon and Lavinia in *Autumn* (ll. 177–310) is saved by its remarkable grace and simplicity. That of Celadon and Amelia in *Summer* (ll. 1169–

1222) may claim indulgence for its comparative beauty ; and it contains some of his best known lines or phrases :

> Each was to each a dearer self,

and

> Or sighed, and looked unutterable things.

But of the longer episode of Damon and Musidora which follows it (ll. 1269–1370) later judgment has been unanimous in disapproval. It was wholly absent from the original *Summer* ; it was introduced in the volume of 1730, but greatly enlarged or rewritten subsequently. Wordsworth's biting (or even venomous) allusion to it as " the passage at which a copy of *The Seasons* will generally be found to open of itself " is not unjust. It can hardly be charged with lubricity, but it is in deplorable taste : it gives some colour to Johnson's dislike and contempt for Thomson. Needless to add, it became a favourite subject for innumerable artists, from Gainsborough downwards, making a good second in popularity to that of Susanna. All three episodes can be detached without leaving any gap ; and one could almost wish that they were.

The Seasons reinstated blank verse as a vehicle, on a large scale, for poetry other than dramatic, and made it thenceforth a form, for the rest of the century and even after, of equal importance and acceptation with the rhymed couplet. Its revival had been started by John Philips, who, after his Miltonic burlesque, *The Splendid Shilling* (1701), had written his equally successful *Cyder* (1708) seriously, as an English Georgic. But it was Thomson who made blank verse universally popular. Without him, it may be doubted whether the *Night Thoughts* or *The Task*, and perhaps even *The Prelude* and *The Excursion* would have taken shape in their actual form. Thomson's versification is based on deep and appreciative study of Milton's. He imitates, as nearly as he can, the Miltonic movement : the periodic structure, the inversions, the Latinisms, the intricate variation of pause, the effects got by sonorous words and rich proper names. His style turns on the *ensemble* of the phrase ; it is a marked feature of it that isolated words are emphasised by abnormal position, mainly at the beginning or end of the phrase. The proportion of lines in *The Seasons* where the end of the phrase and the end of the line coincide is only a little more than one half ; this is in sharp contrast with the *Night Thoughts*, where the proportion is about eight to one, with an effect of extreme and wearying monotony. Thomson also borrcws from the Miltonic diction freely, both in words and phrases. This is not theft. It was then, and may still be, thought no less justifiable than it was frank and unconcealed ; its legitimacy depends on the success with which it is done.

No more than anyone else did Thomson capture the inimitable music. Many passages are rather exercises in the manner than achievements in it ; " the writer's work," as has been said, " sometimes comes near being the fulfilment of a task " ; in the unfailing head of pressure behind the workmanship Milton's blank verse stands alone. But at his best, Thomson comes as near the unapproachable as any one else has done : in his management of the long period, sometimes extending to thirty lines or more, nearer than any one else. But he is at his best where he keeps his rhythms simple and does not attempt too much. Instances need not be multiplied ; but one may be given as typical, the eight lines (*Spring*, ll. 323–330) describing the perpetual spring of an earlier world :

Pure was the temperate air ; an even calm
Perpetual reigned, save what the zephyrs bland

Breathed o'er the blue expanse : for then nor storms
Were taught to blow, nor hurricanes to rage ;
Sound slept the waters ; no sulphureous glooms
Swelled in the sky and sent the lightning forth ;
While sickly damps and cold autumnal fogs
Hung not relaxing on the springs of life.

One metrical device of great effectiveness he took from
Dante—unless it is a mere coincidence and was independ-
ently invented by him.   This is the following up and so
to speak clenching a period by a single separate line
beginning with " and."   It is a favourite device of
Dante's at the end of a canto.   Concluding cadences like

E caddi como corpo morto cade

or

E il pensamento in sogno trasmutai

are familiar to all readers of the *Commedia* ; and they lose
none of their effect when one realises the skilled purpose
behind them.   The same may be said of Thomson's
concluding lines :

And Ocean trembles for his green domain,

or, the line which Wordsworth admired so much,

And Mecca saddens at the long delay.

They close the period in a single massive chord by
which the ear and the imagination are alike satisfied.

In sensitiveness to Nature, and in accuracy both of
observation and of expression, Thomson stood alone in
his age, and has seldom since been equalled, seldomer
still surpassed.   As a landscape artist he ranks with
Tennyson.   His sense of colour and atmosphere, his skill
in selection and composition, are alike remarkable.   His
landscapes have been compared to those of Claude in their
" rich envelopment of light," but this is not carried so far

as to lose touch with truth or impair the feeling of reality.
A line of his,

> The rigid hoar-frost melts before his beam,

familiar to thousands as the motto of Turner's noble
Frosty Morning in the National Gallery, is like the
picture itself in its combination of exact truth to nature
with the highest idealisation. It would be tempting to
enlarge on this quality in his poetry ; but a few instances
in different kinds may be taken out of many ; they may
excite towards further search. Take then, as examples,
the colour and feeling of an English midsummer in

> With-half shut eyes beneath the floating shade
> Of willows grey close-crowding o'er the brook :

the sea, as seen from cliffs or downs on the coast, that

> Far to the blue horizon's utmost verge
> Restless, reflects a floating gleam :

haymakers at work while

> they rake the green appearing ground
> And drive the dusky wave along the mead :

the colour of a bright winter day, when the sun has melted
the snow on the lowlands, but

> His azure gloss the mountain still maintains :

moonrise on a still mild evening, when

> the moon
> Peeps through the chambers of the fleecy East :

and notice in each case the delicate accuracy of the
epithets. Or compare small vivid touches like

> The yellow wallflower stained with iron-brown

and

> Where the breeze blows from yon extended field
> Of blossomed beans :

H

with vast aerial landscapes, like that of the autumnal
bird-migration :

> Infinite wings ! till all the plume-dark air
> And rude resounding shore are one wild cry :

of the Border night-thunderstorm when

> Far seen the heights of heathy Cheviot blaze :

of the melancholy and romantic region where the northern
ocean

> Boils round the naked melancholy isles
> Of furthest Thule, and the Atlantic surge
> Pours in among the stormy Hebrides.

Or again, one might quote, as a typical instance of
the skill with which Thomson combines sensitiveness to
Nature with classical diction and evolution of language
according to a rather academic yet fine tradition, the celebrated description of a summer morning :

> When now no more the alternate Twins are fired
> And Cancer reddens with the solar blaze,
> Short is the doubtful empire of the night ;
> And soon, observant of approaching day,
> The meek-eyed morn appears, mother of dews,
> At first faint-gleaming in the dappled East,
> Till far o'er ether spreads the widening glow
> And from before the lustre of her face
> White break the clouds away.   With quickened step
> Brown night retires.   Young day pours in apace
> And opens all the lawny prospect wide.
> The dripping rock, the mountain's misty top
> Swell on the sight and brighten with the dawn.
> Blue through the dusk the smoking currents shine,
> And from the bladed field the fearful hare
> Limps awkward, while along the forest glade
> The wild deer trip and often turning gaze
> At early passenger.

This, like many other of the best-known passages in the poem, is not free from faults, both those of the period and those peculiar to Thomson himself : the mechanical epithets, the hammering on a particular metrical device until it becomes wearisome (as in the *white, brown, blue* of the ninth, tenth and fourteenth lines), and the verbosity, on which Johnson laid his finger (or his fist) when he said of Thomson, " His fault is such a cloud of words sometimes that the sense can hardly peep through. Shiels, who compiled Cibber's ' Lives of the Poets,' was one day sitting with me. I took down Thomson and read aloud a large portion of him, and then asked, ' Is not this fine ? ' Shiels having expressed the highest admiration, ' Well, Sir,' said I, ' I have omitted every other line.' " Johnson may have been pulling Shiels' leg—or possibly Boswell's. But the criticism is in substance just, and hardly needs labouring for any one who knows *The Seasons*. It is for instance characteristic, or symptomatic, that the paraphrase in *Autumn* of the *O fortunatos nimium* of the Second Georgic dilutes into forty-three lines what Virgil had said in seventeen.

Sensitiveness to sound is no less marked a quality in the *Seasons* than sensitiveness to colour ; and there is the same fineness in rendering it. The lines describing the spring chorus of birds are almost Tennysonian in their discriminating precision :

> The blackbird whistles from the thorny brake,
> The mellow bullfinch answers from the grove,
> Nor are the linnets, o'er the flowery furze
> Poured out profusely, silent.

The approaching thunderstorm is handled with no less truth :

> A boding silence reigns
> Dread through the dun expanse, save the dull sound

> That from the mountain previous to the storm
> Rolls o'er the muttering earth, disturbs the flood
> And shakes the forest leaf without a breath.

And it is not idly that he calls on his Muse

> To swell her note with all the rushing winds,
> To suit her sounding cadence to the floods.

His remarkable accuracy in descriptions of nature goes along with breadth of touch and avoidance of that over-particular detail which is the weakness of Cowper.   His observation is true and discriminating, even when the diction in which it is conveyed is to our ears artificial or obsolete.   There are exceptions to this general rule ; he is not, like Wordsworth or Tennyson, impeccable.   I am sorry to say that, like other poets both before and after him, he makes the planet Venus rise at evening and "unrival'd reign, the fairest lamp of night" until morning. He has two very fine descriptions of moonrise.   One, in *Autumn* (ll. 1088–1102), is faultless in truth of observation, though encumbered with an astronomical parenthesis. The other is in *Winter* : at sunset, he says,

> Rising slow,
> Blank, in the leaden-coloured east, the moon
> Wears a wan circle round her blunted horns.

The moon, when she so rises, is not horned.   It is curious how constantly descriptive writers, both in prose and verse, go wrong about the moon's movements and phases. Even Morris does so, in the lovely opening scene of *The Message of the March Wind*.   In Thomson, it is only surprising because of his usual accuracy.

As regards the artificiality of his diction, it must always be remembered that much of what seems stiff or mannered or unsuited for poetry now, need not have been so, and was not so, then.   The use of language suffers a

slow secular change.   When Milton, in one of the loveliest of his lyrics, makes the Attendant Spirit say

And not many furlongs hence
Is your Father's residence,

the concluding word gives us a slight shock ; then, it was
a stately word, almost equivalent to *palace*, and exactly
descriptive of Ludlow Castle as the seat of the Lord-
President of Wales.   The same applies to many of what
seem the unpoetical words of the Augustans ; " previous
to the storm," quoted above, is an instance.

The age disliked neologisms, and sought effects, as
Horace also had done in the Odes, by ingenious combi-
nations of very simple words.   Thomson does this habitually, and often admirably.   But he repeats his effects
too much ; hence the feeling that he tends to give, in
continuous reading, of monotony and declamation.   Nor
is it possible to acquit him of the anxiety for dignity, the
souci du style noble which has recourse to periphrases.

Among points of diction characteristic of, though not
peculiar to Thomson, is to be noted his large use of
compound epithets.   In these he is often, though not
always, felicitous.   He extended the compass of the
language by them ; they come on almost every page of
The Seasons.   Some, like *meek-eyed*, which was attacked at
the time, and *rosy-bosomed*, he took from Milton, some
from the older poets : the greater number seem to be of
his own coinage.   With his *dewy-bright*—which Pope
wished to alter into *bright with dew*—it is interesting to
compare Tennyson's *dewy-dark* in *Œnone*.   Among the
most successful are *hollow-whispering*, which he uses
twice ; *many-twinkling*, stolen from him by Gray in the
Progress of Poesy ; and *dim-discovered*, to which a new
beauty of setting was given by Collins in the *Ode to
Evening*.   The passage where it occurs in *The Seasons*

deserves quotation, not only for its own sake, but for comparison with Tennyson's treatment of the same motive, the shipwrecked sailor in tropical seas :

> Day after day,
> Sad on the jutting eminence he sits
> And views the main that ever toils below ;
> Still fondly forming in the farthest verge
> Where the round ether mixes with the wave
> Ships, dim-discovered, dropping from the clouds.
> At evening to the setting sun he turns
> A mournful eye, and down his dying heart
> Sinks helpless, while the wonted roar is up
> And hiss continual through the tedious night.

The twenty-eight lines of gorgeous description beginning " The mountain wooded to the peak " in *Enoch Arden* into which Tennyson expanded the motive are so well known that they need not be cited in full.   It is interesting to note that they contain three of the compound epithets to which both poets are so partial, *league-long, seaward-gazing, hollower-bellowing*.   And the main point is that it may be fairly said that Thomson does not suffer from the comparison ; it is the modern poet here who may be thought overwrought and over-coloured.

Another small matter of diction is interesting enough to notice in passing ; Thomson's curious fondness for adjectives ending in *-ive*.   Of these I have counted about forty in *The Seasons* ; there may be more.   They come so frequently as to give a colour to the style, and there is no doubt that they tend to jar on the modern reader.   As a study in the growth and use of language, to analyse the list would be a curious and perhaps not an unprofitable enquiry.   They fall roughly under three heads :

First, those fully assimilated into the English language and used freely in poetry and prose alike : such are *plaintive, sportive, attentive, expressive, pensive, passive*.

All but one of these six occur in Shakespeare ; three in Milton.   Their use provokes no comment.

Secondly, those which were originally formed for poetical use, but have since become restricted to prose, and many of them to purely technical usage.   Among these are *progressive* and *inquisitive* (both occurring in Milton), *vegetative, protective, adhesive, infusive* ; *comprehensive* was reinstated in poetical diction, with doubtful success, by Tennyson.

Thirdly, those more or less decisively rejected by the genius of the language, now hardly used at all, and even if they are, regarded as inadmissible in poetry.   Such are two of Thomson's favourite words, *amusive* and *diffusive* ; such are *conjunctive* and *directive*, which are both used by Shakespeare, and *concoctive*, which is used by Milton ; such *prelusive* and *inexhaustive*, which reappear, anomalously, in the poetry of Wordsworth and Southey.

Thomson, as I have said, was a diligent student of the older poets, and a skilful borrower or adapter from them. Himself he has similarly been a rich quarry for his successors.   Throughout the rest of the eighteenth century this is patent ; but it did not cease there. One may mention two or three surprising instances. Coleridge's famous and much-debated

> The western sky
> And its peculiar tint of yellow green

derives from Thomson's

> How clear the cloudless sky, how deeply tinged
> With a peculiar blue.

In Wordsworth's magical

> Lady of the Lake
> Sole-sitting by the shores of old romance,

sole-sitting is one of Thomson's compound epithets. And more curiously still, in Keats' sonnet *On First looking into Chapman's Homer* the expression *wild-surmise* is taken from Thomson ; and not from *The Seasons*, but from the dreary and laboured *Liberty*.

And if later poets have thus plundered him freely, we find in him, conversely, remarkable anticipations of poets who came long after him.

> Devoting all
> To love, each was to each a dearer self,
> Supremely happy in the awakened power
> Of giving joy :
>
> The clouds commixed
> With stars swift-gliding sweep along the sky :

these lines are not Wordsworth's, but Thomson's, though they are exactly what Wordsworth would have written. Thomson's too, though anybody might say at once "Tennyson" if asked who was the author, are

> Taught him to chip the wood and hew the stone,

or

> The talk
> Vociferous at once from twenty tongues
> Reels fast from theme to theme, from horses, hounds,
> To Church or mistress, politics or ghost :

and it was Thomson who remarked and recorded the apples " falling frequent through the chiller night " a century before Tennyson wrote *The Lotos-Eaters*.

There is more in this than mere curiosity. It makes us realise more vividly that English poetry is a continuous movement ; and also, a point on which stress must be laid, that Thomson is on the central line of its course more even than was his greater contemporary, Pope.

For Londoners, he has a further special interest, as the

poet most closely associated with a neighbourhood as rich
in natural beauty as in literary associations.   It is needless to catalogue the names which cluster round the reach
of the Thames from Twickenham to Kew—a landscape
of still unrivalled beauty in spite of all that over-popula-
tion has done, and does daily, to spoil and vulgarise it.
Thomson made its acquaintance soon after he came to
London from Scotland in 1725 : he loved and frequented
it more and more ; and in the spring of 1736 settled in
it for the rest of his life.   " Please to direct to me," he
writes to Hill early in May of that year, " in Kew Lane,
Richmond, Surrey, and order your letters to be put into
the General Post."   Kew Lane was a straggling country
road, that ran from Richmond to Kew through meadows
and orchards, past Lord Capel's celebrated garden of
eleven acres, the germ out of which Kew Gardens has
since grown.   The fragment left of it, now called Kew
Foot Lane, passes from behind Richmond Station along
by the Old Deer Park and the entrance to the Athletic
Grounds.   It is still a pretty little backwater, with a row
of late seventeenth-century houses almost intact, and a
public-house whose name, the Tulip Tree, has a fine old-
fashioned flavour.   Whether it replaces the Old Orange
Tree to which Thomson used to go for convivial evenings
with Quin the actor and other friends, I am unable to
ascertain.   Some of the structure of his cottage or villa
(it is mentioned by both names) is said to remain embedded
in the Royal Hospital where it fronts the Deer Park.
But even the older part of the frontage is much later ;
the rest of the building is modern, and its extension has
left only a scrap of Thomson's garden.   His cottage was
all on one floor.   It was still there in 1805 ; then it
passed into the hands of Lord Shaftesbury, who enlarged
or rebuilt it.   The Countess Dowager of Shaftesbury,

widow of the seventh Earl, died there in 1866 ; and the conversion of the premises into a hospital was made soon afterwards.

That whole neighbourhood was one of exceptional beauty, even at a time when all the surroundings of London were beautiful ; when Notting Hill and St. John's Wood were actual forests, Hampstead a sequestered upland ; Paddington, Chelsea, Kensington, Islington isolated country villages. The rich woods, the noble river, the " pleasant cottages and farms," the stately country-houses of which one or two, like Ham House and Montrose House, still remain, gave it every variety of charm. Richmond Park was already then a century old ; the quiet little town of Richmond lay below, clustered round the Green and the derelict Tudor Palace, and straggling up the long hill. It would be a good day's pleasuring even now to start from Kew Foot Lane with a copy of *The Seasons* in one's pocket—or, still better perhaps, with *The Seasons* in one's head—and follow up the author's wanderings. Though fat and indolent, he was an indefatigable pedestrian, and thought nothing of walking both ways between his cottage and London. That walk can hardly now be recommended for pleasure. But any one who started on the expedition from London on a summer day might well begin it by going up by water to Kew from the Doves at Hammersmith, as Thomson was also fond of doing. Chiswick, Mortlake, Strand-on-the-Green, all preserve on their river-frontages a good deal of the aspect, and some of the actual buildings, of his time. From the site of his cottage, the first walk to take would be up to the view described with loving minuteness and fine breadth of handling in what is probably the most celebrated passage of the poem, that beginning, *Wherefore should we choose ?* The lines (*Summer*, 1402–1466) are too long to quote—and it may be hoped that to quote them would be superfluous. Or, if a spring morning were chosen for the expedition, his invitation may be recalled :

> Now from the town
> Buried in smoke and sleep and noisome damps
> Oft let me wander o'er the dewy fields
> Where freshness breathes, and dash the trembling drops
> From the bent bush, as through the verdant maze
> Of sweet-briar hedges I pursue my walk :

or if an autumn afternoon, once more :

> But see, the fading many-coloured woods,
> Shade deepening over shade, the country round
> Imbrown : a crowded umbrage, dusk and dun.
> Meantime, light-shadowing all, a sober calm
> Fleeces unbounded ether, whose least wave
> Stands tremulous, uncertain where to turn
> The gentle current ; while, illumined wide,
> The dewy-skirted clouds imbibe the sun.

In August 1748 Thomson had gone up to London from Kew—probably to his favourite resort, Slaughter's Coffee-house in Covent Garden—and started to walk back according to his habit. At Hammersmith he found himself tired, and took boat at the Doves. On the water he caught a severe chill ; it developed next day into what, in the careless nomenclature of the time, is called a fever—probably pneumonia—and after a partial rally, he succumbed to it a few days later. He was just forty-eight.

He was buried in Richmond Church, under a plain stone ; the brass tablet was only put up in 1792, by his admirer the eccentric eleventh Earl of Buchan. The Adam monument in Westminster Abbey had been erected thirty years earlier. But his best monument is Collins' exquisite ode, *In yonder grave a Druid lies*,

written soon after his death, which will last as long as the
English language.   Second to it are Burns' beautiful
stanzas, written at Buchan's request in 1791 for the
annual commemoration of Thomson in his native parish
of Ednam.   " Who would write after Collins ? " Burns
said with modest self-depreciation.   " I read over his
verses and despaired.   I attempted three or four stanzas,
which will, I am afraid, be too convincing a proof how
unequal I am to the task."   The annual Ednam celebration went on for nearly thirty years more ; when it
ceased, Burns had himself replaced Thomson in the
idolising affection of his fellow-countrymen.

Of Thomson's immense fame, both in England and
on the Continent, for generations after his death, it is
needless to speak in detail.   He had his detractors ; and
as we have seen, much of his work gave an easy handle to
detraction.   Johnson's valuation of him is grudging.
Perhaps Johnson was influenced in this by Savage,
to whom Thomson had always been kind and helpful,
and who always bit the hand that fed him.   Modern
research has cleared Thomson's character from aspersion,
and brought him out as uniformly generous and lovable,
with no fault beyond indolence—as Lyttelton quaintly
said of him, " he loathed much to write "—and a rather
excessive love of good eating.   He has been called,
depreciatingly, " the poet of the cultivated middle class " :
this is, so far as it goes, true.   *The Seasons* remained for
a long time the most popular single poem in the English
language ; next to it perhaps, but for a shorter period
and to a narrower circle, came the *Night Thoughts*.   Both
had a European reputation, and a most powerful effect
both on the naturalistic and on the romantic movement
of the century.   They were almost as well known in
France as in England.   Already in 1730 Voltaire " had

discovered in him a great genius " ; and twenty years later wrote of him in generous praise to Lyttelton, who was then engaged on the incredible task—fortunately dropped by him before publication—of re-writing *The Seasons* with the view of removing everything in the poem which smelt of unorthodoxy or which failed to satisfy his own ideas of elegance and dignity. He was no less ardently admired by minds so different, and moving over so wide a range, as Montesquieu, Rousseau, and Madame Roland. Writing from prison during the Terror, Madame Roland quotes from *The Seasons* verses *que je ne répète jamais sans attendrissement* : they are from the apostrophe to Winter :

> Pleased have I wandered through your rough domain,
> Trod the pure virgin snows, myself as pure,
> Heard the winds roar and the big torrent burst
> Or seen the deep-fermenting tempest brewed
> In the dim evening sky.

They strike that new note the reverberations of which were to revolutionise the world.

Johnson, with all his dislike of Thomson, is candid enough to say, " he had a true poetical genius." Wordsworth, while censuring him for vicious style, false ornaments, and sentimental commonplace, adds words that, coming from him, mean much, and that outweigh all adverse criticism, " Thomson was an inspired poet." If he is less read and less admired now, the fault is not his ; and the loss is ours.

EDWARD YOUNG

A Lecture given at the Royal Society of
Literature, 24 April 1918

EDWARD YOUNG

Any appreciation of English literature would be incomplete which did not take some account of spent fames—of those names which had immense vogue in their own time or beyond it, and then sank, as it seems irretrievably, into practical oblivion. I do not mean the mere comets of a season—those authors or books that have their six months of popularity, only to set, *desti e spenti*, as quickly as they rose. What I mean is writings which have made their mark for, and upon, a whole generation, and, in virtue of doing so, have " earned a place i' the story." They have had a substantial and ponderable share in moulding thought, in determining taste, in giving, for the period of their influence, a bias to thought and its expression ; and thus they have been factors towards shaping the way in which life has actually been regarded and a pattern of life has been drawn. Then their period has come to its term ; they have ceased, as it appears, to live.

Such spent fames are dotted at intervals over the course of poetry, and it is an interesting speculation whether the submergence is, in any case, final, as, in some cases, it is not. Shakespeare's *Sonnets*, to take one amazing instance, were all but forgotten, or named only to be slighted, for more than a hundred and fifty years. Perhaps it can never be said with complete certainty of any poetry which has once kindled enthusiasm and won fame

I

that it has passed irrecoverably to the realm of things for-gotten. But instances are not wanting where a long and wide success—and that of a quality so high that it may properly be called fame—burned itself away, sank into its embers, and has become, so far as we can judge or fore-see, extinct. In the seventeenth century Quarles and Cowley had successively such a fame beyond all their con-temporaries ; and among those contemporaries was Milton. Cowley indeed effectually survives by the few pieces which are transcribed in all anthologies ; he may be counted one of the lesser immortals. Quarles' *Emblems* continued to be re-read and reprinted well into the nineteenth century, but the bulk of his poetry (and that bulk is very large) was already dead when Pope gibbeted his name in a scornful half-line. Who now, except a professional student of literature, knows or reads the epics by which Southey, and many of Southey's contem-poraries, fancied that he had secured imperishable fame ? Who now has the curiosity to disinter, or the patience to peruse, the tragedies by which Joanna Baillie, in the partial judgment of Scott, had taken a place only a little below Shakespeare ? For nearly a generation after its first appearance in 1839, the *Festus* of another Bailey, Philip James, was the most widely read and the most admired poem of its age ; it is only known now by being made, at rare intervals, the subject of a paper by some curious student of the byways and back-alleys of literature.

Among these spent fames Edward Young has long been reckoned. His popularity was not only very great, but was of long duration. The *Night Thoughts*, during the latter half of the eighteenth century and well into the nineteenth, ran through edition after edition. They were to be found in every library—almost, one might say, in every household. They formed a school. Their influence was immense, not only in England, but on the Continent. They provided journalism, and even familiar language, with numberless passages or phrases for habitual use. Now, and for a long time back, they have effectively existed only in quotations, a number of which are still in daily currency, though few, perhaps, who use them know their origin. They lie stranded like seaweed or jelly-fish on a shore from which the tide has long retreated. The title of the *Night Thoughts*, though not the work itself, is indeed still familiar ; it was one of Young's many happy coinages. But of Young's other works, some of which were also in their time famous, hardly even the names are known beyond the circle of professed and specialising students.

Young was not unfortunate in his chroniclers and critics any more than in the success of his poetry with the public. The biography by Croft, of which Johnson thought so well that he inserted it bodily in his " Lives of the Poets," is an able piece of work, in a spirited yet not servile imitation of the Johnsonian manner. To it Johnson himself added half a dozen pages of his own finest, surest-handed, and most penetrating criticism. That was when Young's fame was still at its height. And it remained high for fifty years more. Mitford's elegant edition of his " Selected Poetical Works," with a new biographical and critical study gracefully and adequately written, was published by Pickering in his Aldine Classics in 1834. It was then still possible to describe him as " one whose works have placed him in the first rank of genius among our English poets." But this was the last monument erected to a fame which was by then on the wane.

Some twenty years later, George Eliot's able and acrid essay, published in the *Westminster Review* under the title of "Worldliness and Other-Worldliness" just before she quitted the trade of criticism for that of novel-writing, dealt what for the time was a fatal blow to his reputation without exciting any great measure of renewed interest in his work. It was a time when the Victorian reaction against the eighteenth century was at its height, very much as the counter-reaction against Victorianism is now. George Eliot's heavy-handed flogging of a dead horse is interesting now rather for the light it throws on her own mind and that of her age than as intelligent or illuminating criticism of the mind and age with which she was dealing.

Only in recent years has the task of exhumation been undertaken by a new adventurer. The discovery by the Historical Manuscripts Commission, among the archives at Longleat, of the letters written by Young over a space of some five and twenty years to Margaret, Duchess of Portland—Prior's "lovely Peggy," the granddaughter of Harley—revived interest in their author and threw a fresh and pleasing light on his character. Stimulated by them and by further unpublished matter in the British Museum and elsewhere to which they directed attention, Mr. H. C. Shelley, four years ago, brought out his interesting volume, "The Life and Letters of Edward Young," which is indispensable for any just appreciation of the man, or even of his work.

The words which Mr. Shelley quotes from Johnson on his title-page, "a man of genius and a poet," are the phrase with which Johnson's own just and fine estimate concludes. They are preceded, however, by the words— which Mr. Shelley does not quote—"with all his defects." These defects have, in fact, proved fatal, and they may be summed up in the acute saying which long before had dropped in conversation from Pope, that Young was "without common sense." But common sense was not

the appanage of the eighteenth or any other century ; it
is, at all times and in all places, a rare individual gift.

So far has an author once famous been left stranded
by the receding tide that, even to an educated audience,
it may not be superfluous to point out, in summary,
Young's curiously unplaced position in that period of
English literary history which is covered by his lifetime.
Of him it may be said, as is said with fuller truth of Gray,
that he was a misfit.   He belongs to no precise period or
school.   By date of birth and in respect of his earlier work
—though even that was not the work of youth, but of an
age which may be called mature—he is one of the
Augustans.   He was one of the circle of wits at Button's,
younger than Swift or Addison, but older than Pope.
Had he died between fifty and sixty, he would be cursorily
noted as one of the Augustan school—the author of moral
and religious poems and of occasional pieces in the formal
manner of that period, but of most mark as a tragedian
and satirist.   The Satires of 1725–28 form a collected
volume of no little brilliance, not unworthy to be placed
beside those of Pope himself, though they lack the
exquisite artist's touch and the faculty of concentration
and distilment.   They are the sources, like his other
works, of celebrated quotations :

A fool at forty is a fool indeed.

For who does nothing with a better grace ?

For her own breakfast she'll project a scheme,
Nor take her tea without a stratagem.

Ruffhead (1769) boldly says (in answer to Warton) that
Young's satire on women is better than Pope's ; but in a
note, half withdraws.   In some sense that is true.   It is
less powerful, but less vicious.

Two of his three full-dress tragedies were produced

with success at Drury Lane, and are not more dead now than Addison's *Cato*. One of these indeed, *The Revenge*, was really popular, and was actually revived by Kemble as far down as 1814, nearly a century after its first production.

This period of Young's literary life ended when he took orders in 1727. Then followed a long period of silence and submergence, during which the Augustan age fulfilled its term. Pope and Swift, its last representatives, died in 1744 and 1745 respectively. The completion, in 1742, of the *Dunciad* in its final form marks the end of the Augustan age in letters and the triumph of that reign of dullness so magnificently set forth in Pope's matchless ending.

It was in that same year that Young broke his long silence. The *Night Thoughts* were published, in seven successive instalments, between 1742 and 1746. They immediately made for their author a new and immensely heightened fame. In that dismal period of English poetry they stood almost alone. When the first four *Nights* were published as a collected volume it ran through six editions in six months. The success of the other five was hardly less. For many years thereafter their circulation and popularity were hardly less than those of the great Augustans themselves. In the new *genre* which he had invented, Young stood without a rival ; for Blair's *Grave* (1743) rather reinforced, than came into competition with, the *Night Thoughts*. Both works effectively survive, indirectly rather than in substance, through Blake's famous designs made sixty years afterwards. But in the long intervening period their popularity had remained undiminished.

Just then poetry was beginning to prepare for a great new departure. Alongside of the feebler post-Augustans

like Akenside or Mallet, the lyrical impulse and the
romantic spirit were pushing out their first tentative
growth.   Collins published his *Odes* in the year in which
the *Night Thoughts* were completed ; Gray's *Eton Ode*
followed in the next year ; and Thomson's *Castle of
Indolence* in the next year again.   From that time on we
are in the period of mixed conservatism and innovation
which is of such fascinating interest and which leads on,
through Warton, Percy, Blake, Cowper, Crabbe, Burns,
to the new age and the poetical revolution consummated
by the *Lyrical Ballads* in 1798.

In virtue of this central work, produced between his
fifty-ninth and sixty-third year, Young may almost be
said to represent a period of his own, alongside of, but
apart from, the general movement—which, indeed, was
just then, except for a few faint first-beginnings, less a
movement than a stagnation.   There is a sort of fantastic
resemblance in this respect between him and Milton.
Milton, like Young, belonged by date and by his earlier
work to a definite period in English poetry.   Like
Young's, his muse kept silence throughout middle life.
Only at the age of sixty, when most poets either have died
or have done their work in poetry, did each break out anew
and produce his masterpiece.   To speak of the *Night
Thoughts* in the same day with the *Paradise Lost* would, of
course, be absurd ; Young's whole work, first and last,
was on a totally different level from that of the most perfect of English poets.   Yet the analogy, so far as it goes,
and the homelessness, as we may call it, of both writers in
their age, remain striking and interesting.

And even this was not all.   Twenty years later still, at
the age of nearly eighty, this singular plant of interrupted
growth and unaccountable fecundity put forth a last
flower.   That poem, *Resignation*, is wholly unique as an

essay at so advanced an age in an entirely new manner. It is the manner, to a considerable extent, of Cowper, and probably owes (as Cowper does) a good deal to the growing prestige of the hymn as a recognised form of poetry. Smart's *Song to David* is of almost the same date. The Wesleys' hymns had been published, and had immediately come into wide use, a good many years earlier. The prolongation of the hymn structure and movement, in this poem of Young's old age, through a piece of no less than 1640 lines, is in one way its own condemnation, in another makes the piece at all events a sufficiently remarkable *tour de force*. Young never, from his earliest work to his latest, knew when to stop ; that was the most obvious mark of the defect noted in him by Pope. But in spite of all the drawbacks which Young here deliberately incurred by this enormous diffusion and fatiguing repetition, *Resignation* preserves throughout a high standard of workmanship ; and, at its best, has a combination of elasticity, precision, and dignity which recalls the work of other and greater poets, and which, in particular, remarkably anticipates the work of a hundred years later. It is hardly possible to read it without being reminded of the austere precision of Matthew Arnold (who also, curiously enough, wrote a poem called *Resignation*). Often one might hesitate, if suddenly confronted with a stanza, to say whether it were from Young's *Resignation* or from Arnold's *Obermann*. Of the six which follow here, three are Young's, three Arnold's ; it would be interesting to know how many readers could at once, or without hesitation, say which are which.

> No martyr e'er defied the flames
>   By stings of life unvext ;
> First rose some quarrel with this world,
>   Then passion for the next.

For he pursued a lonely road
   His eyes on Nature's plan ;
Neither made man too much a God
   Nor God too much a man.

With hope extinct and brow composed
   I marked the present die ;
Its term of life was nearly closed,
   Yet it had more than I.

Heaven's choice is safer than our own ;
   Of ages past inquire
What the most formidable fate ?
   To have our own desire.

Dispute you this ?   O stand in awe
   And cease your sorrow : know
That tears now trickling down He saw
   Ten thousand years ago.

We in some unknown Power's employ
   Move on a rigorous line ;
Can neither, when we will, enjoy,
   Nor, when we will, resign.

But here and there, even in his earlier work, Young
had anticipated the handling and colour of other modern
poets also. Lines in the *Night Thoughts* like—

   A riddle then ! Have patience ; I'll explain,

or,

   If man's immortal, there's a God in heaven,

have a quality which in its impatient colloquialism, its
eagerness to get at the point, is characteristic of Browning.
   Such was the range and variety of Young's poetry, extending as it did over a space of nearly fifty years, from
before the death of Queen Anne until after the accession
of George III. It was work which is never discreditable,
except in his occasional disastrous attempts at what in that
age was called the Ode. Few and evil were his lyrics.

" He seems to have been under some malignant influence," Johnson aptly remarks, whenever he attempted them ; they are below the level, if that be possible, of the common hack-work of their period.   Except in them, his verse is generally meritorious, often excellent, and now and then really rising to greatness or flashing into beauty. Nor can it be called imitative in any sense of special depreciation.   Derivative it is, like much good poetry, and in some sense like nearly all poetry whether good or bad. He took the colour of his models, but his models were classics, ancient or modern.   His open thefts may be defended on the ground of their very obviousness.   The many passages which he has enriched, as other and greater poets have also done, by transference of whole phrases from the *Paradise Lost*, whatever judgment may be formed of them on other grounds, do not break any canon of literary ethics.   For Milton was to him (as to Wordsworth later) one of the classics, and might be used like a Greek or Latin poet.   These borrowings are on the same footing as those to which no exception is ever taken ; like the line in the *Night Thoughts* translated, and very beautifully translated, from Callimachus,

How often we talked down the summer's sun !

or the other, a literal rendering of Lucretius,

Beyond the flaming limits of the world,

or, from Lucretius again, but this time not so closely or so successfully,

Birth's feeble cry, and death's deep dismal groan.

But he has generally, and in all his characteristic work, a very distinct quality of his own.   The trouble is, that this quality is not good enough.   In poetry, as in all art, the difference between the first-rate and the second-rate is not one of degree, but of kind and essence.

In any detailed criticism of the *Night Thoughts* we have to discriminate carefully between lines and passages of real beauty and splendour, and others which are merely grandiose at the best, or which, still oftener, are resounding platitudes and sometimes—too often !—flat absurdities.

No lapse of time or change of taste can dim lines like

> God's image disinherited of day,

or,

> The melancholy ghosts of dead renown,

or the noble phrase of

> Godhead streaming through a thousand worlds.

No imagination can cease to thrill to the compressed force or stately rhetoric of his argument where it rises highest :

> Time flies, death urges, knells call, heaven invites,
> Hell threatens.

> His grief is but his grandeur in disguise,
> And discontent is immortality.

> O condescend to think as angels think !
> O tolerate a chance for happiness !

> Why this so sumptuous insult o'er our heads ?
> Why this illustrious canopy displayed ?
> Why so magnificently lodged despair ?

There need be no hesitation, and little, if any, qualification, in praise of passages so admirable as

> Beneath
> Aerial groves' impenetrable gloom,
> Or in some mighty ruin's solemn shade,
> Or gazing by pale lamps on high-born dust
> In vaults, thin courts of poor unflattered kings ;

or

> Where is the dust that has not been alive ?
> The spade, the plough, disturb our ancestors,
> From human mould we reap our daily bread ;

or the celebrated vision of the world before the deluge,

>   Of one departed world
> I see the mighty shadow : oozy wreath
> And dismal seaweed crown her : o'er her urn
> Reclined, she weeps her desolated realms
> And bloated sons, and, weeping, prophesies
> Another's dissolution, soon, in flames :

or the succinct and brilliant epitome of the *Praeparatio Evangelica*, where, for once forgetting to be diffuse and to repeat himself, he puts into nine crowded yet lucid and rapid lines the substance of a whole volume :

> The world was made ; was ruined ; was restored :
> Laws from the sky were published, were repealed :
> On earth kings, kingdoms rose ; kings, kingdoms fell.
> Famed sages lighted up the pagan world :
> Prophets from Sion darted a keen glance
> Through distant age ; saints travelled ; martyrs bled ;
> By wonders sacred nature stood controlled ;
> The living were translated, dead were raised ;
> Angels and more than angels came from heaven.

On a wholly different footing are those passages of sententious and glittering rhetoric by which Young is best known, through their having been for generations the stock commonplaces of preachers or moralists :

> A deity believed is joy begun,
> A deity adored is joy advanced,
> A deity beloved is joy matured ;

or,

> Heaven gives us friends to bless the present scene,
> Resumes them, to prepare us for the next.

When he is in this vein, Young not merely ceases to be

a poet ; he makes any lover of poetry feel sick.   Elsewhere, disgust is mingled with amusement :

> He weeps, the falling drop puts out the sun.
>
>   The tears pumped up by death
> Are spent in watering vanities of life.
>
> In an eternity, what scenes shall strike !
> Adventures thicken ! novelties surprise !
>
> The world's a system of theology :

this last oddly like Browning again, and still liker Mrs.
Browning ; it ought to be, and something very like it is,
in *Aurora Leigh*.   And it passes into almost unqualified
amusement when Young's sententiousness, as it often
does, sinks into sheer bathos :

> A Christian is the highest style of man.
>
> O'er friends deceased full heartily she wept.
>
> And is Lorenzo's salamander-heart
> Cold and untouched amidst these sacred fires ?

or in the little-known apostrophe which precedes the well-
known line, " An undevout astronomer is mad,"

> Devotion ! daughter of astronomy !

   The search after sententiousness, the constant effort to
be striking at whatever cost, is Young's besetting vice.
In this respect, as in others, he may be called the English
Seneca.   He resembles Seneca, too, in his endless flux
of words.   He is never content to make his point and
have done.   Even where (as is often the case) he has hit the
nail on the head, he goes on with a shower of rattling
blows, which are quite ineffective, and only serve to
fatigue the reader and to impair the force of the first
stroke.   The result in detail is a ᴛendency to anti-climax
so persistent that it might be called systematic ; in the

total large effect, it is an amount of repetition which in a
sermon might be excused or even justified, but in a poem
is insufferable.   There is a familiar and apparently authentic story of Young once preaching before George II.
" Finding His Majesty very inattentive, he raised his
voice very much, and when this had no effect, burst into
tears."   In the *Night Thoughts* he is always raising his
voice very much, but goes obstinately on ; and the sense
of fatigue grows.   The later *Nights* contain many of his
finest lines and passages ; yet the effective value of the
whole, as well as its chances of life, would have been
greater had he stopped at the end of the fourth *Night,*
or possibly even sooner.   But he was without common
sense.

Indeed, the *Night Thoughts* are often—to modern taste
and modern impatience are habitually—little more than
sermons hammered by main force into verse : as he says
himself of them, in what is an effort towards self-criticism,
though put into the mouth of an imaginary opponent,

Truths which at church you might have heard in prose.

His letters show him as, what we might not otherwise
suspect, human, kindly, not without quiet humour in
spite of that pomposity of diction in which he bettered
the example of his age.   Sometimes, even in his poetry,
it is permissible to doubt whether he is perfectly serious.
When he tells us that—

Punctual as lovers to the moment sworn
I keep my assignation with my woe ;

that

'Tis time, high time, to shift this dismal scene ;

or when he says of God (whom he generally prefers, as
was   the   current   fashion,   to   call   by   such   names   as

" Eternity's inhabitant august," or " the great immutable,"
or " the mighty dramatist "),

> He tunes
> My voice (if tuned),

is there anything in his tone and language beyond colossal
fatuity ? Perhaps ; but more probably not.

Even his " quotations," those single lines which have
gained universal currency, tell more when detached than
in their context, which, indeed, oftener than not impairs
their effectiveness. On their separate brilliance it is
needless to enlarge ; the mere fact of their survival is all
the testimony they need, as the fact that their source is
generally forgotten is the index to Young's general failure
in poetic vitality. It is probable that five people out of
six, if asked where

> Tired Nature's sweet restorer, balmy Sleep

came from, would answer, " Shakespeare." At all
events, as few would know it for the opening line of the
Night Thoughts as would know a line almost as celebrated,

> Music hath charms to soothe the savage breast,

for the opening line of *The Mourning Bride*.

But almost on every other page one comes on a famous
line :

> We take no note of time but from its loss.
>
> Where is to-morrow ? in another world.
>
> Be wise to-day ; 'tis madness to defer,

followed, characteristically, after two intervening lines of
feeble verbiage in the same sense, by the still more famous
crystallisation,

> Procrastination is the thief of time.
>
> At thirty, man suspects himself a fool.

(The equally well-known lines which follow, and that pursue the course of human life, invite and almost demand quotation :

> Knows it at forty, and reforms his plan ;
> At fifty, chides his infamous delay ;
> Pushes his prudent purpose to resolve ;
> In all the magnanimity of thought
> Resolves and re-resolves ; then dies the same.)

All men think all men mortal but themselves.

That hideous sight, a naked human heart.

Truth never was indebted to a lie.

One sun by day, by night ten thousand shine.

Or, one of the most noticeable and interesting of all,

> Man wants but little, nor that little long.

Twenty-three years later, that line won its immortality : it ceased to be Young's and became Goldsmith's. He took it bodily, and with one deft stroke of that hand which touched nothing that it did not adorn, gave it translucency, made it sing. The famous stanza has that lovely melody, that incomparable sweetness, in which Goldsmith has no equal or second in his century, whether he be using a lyric measure or writing in what is technically the heroic couplet of the Augustans :

> Then, pilgrim, turn, thy cares forgo ;
> All earth-born cares are wrong.
> Man wants but little here below,
> Nor wants that little long.

"Out of the eater came forth meat, and out of the strong came forth sweetness."

I do not propose—and time would not serve—to enter here into Young's metrical technique. In the art of blank verse he may fairly be called one of the Little

Masters.   The versification in the *Night Thoughts*, while
heavy, even stiff, is skilful and dignified—something in
the manner of early Georgian architecture.   At its best,
as some of the passages I have cited show, it is very good
indeed ; at its worst it is monotonously mechanical ; on
its ordinary level it lacks modulation, its musical phrasing
is poor, and he hammers on the keys.   But in this the
metrical structure does but follow the evolution of the
thought.   Both are rhetorical rather than imaginative,
and in both the rhetoric is formal and often pedantic.
Yet a greater sincerity of technique might be claimed for
Young's blank verse, stiff and heavy as it is, than there
is in the elaborate and equally artificial modulation of the
blank verse in Thomson's *Seasons*.   There is something
to be said for not even attempting the large, fluid, periodic
movement where it does not come naturally, but is only a
clever imitative artifice.

   It was as a moral or theological rather than as a poetical
work that the *Night Thoughts* had their main success in
their own age and country.   The whole poem is, or purports to be, a refutation of atheism and a vindication of
Christianity.   Young's theological system is, indeed,
neither profound nor coherent.   He fluctuates between
rationalistic Deism and doctrine, little, if at all, removed
from that of the Methodist revival.   " Rewards and
punishments make God adored " is the essence of his
doctrine, but that was a doctrine then generally prevalent
except among mystics or extreme predestinarians.   In
his theology he was of his age, neither worse nor better ;
in his art his theory was superior to his practice.   " Be
not concerned about Lovelace," he writes to Richardson
in 1744 ; " 'tis the likeness, not the morality, of a character we call for."   But his own characters, if they may
be called such—his Lorenzo, Philander, Florello, Aspasia,

K

Narcissa, Calista—have no likeness " distinguishable in
member, joint, or limb." They are merely, like Hervey's
Theron and Aspasio, labels on abstractions, and most of
them had, in fact, already appeared as such in his *Satires*.

But his European fame was hardly less than his fame
among his own countrymen, and it was based on grounds
which had certainly nothing to do with religion and as
little with morals. He was the initiator and protagonist
of one side of the romantic movement ; he at once stimulated and satisfied what French critics call *le goût du
sombre*. Even before his time this was recognised abroad
as an English characteristic—*un feu sombre*, says Resnel
in 1730. It culminated in the mid-century. Hervey's
Meditations among the Tombs, which was published in the
same year (1745) as the last but one of the *Nights*, ran
them hard in popularity, and passed through twenty-five
editions before the French Revolution. The Anglo-
mania which began in France under the Regency and
continued for half a century took many forms, and this
was one of the most pervasive. Its after-effects remain
strong even in the Romantic movement of 1830. But
in the generation which immediately followed the appearance of the *Night Thoughts*, *le genre sombre*, both in
literature and largely in art—particularly in the art of
illustration—swept over France, and from France over
Europe. *La tristesse des Nuits* was a passion. Richardson, Young, and Ossian were the great trinity of models,
and Young's prestige was scarcely less than that of
Richardson. Poets aspired to be *l'Young Français*.
Digne d'Young et de Shakespeare is a phrase quite seriously
used by Restif de la Bretonne. Le Tourneur's translation (1760) ran through edition after edition. It was
embellished with the no less popular engravings which
set a fashion for half a century, and in which the main

ingredients are a tomb, moonlight, a skull, a lantern, yews or cypresses, a man of sensibility striking an attitude, and, if possible, a sheeted corpse. The original edition of the first *Night* had itself been adorned by a portrait of the author meditating in a moonlit churchyard. Libraries in old country houses are seldom without specimens of this type of art. It was still popular when, just about the turn of the century, Jane Austen ran her delicate point into it. All English readers know the sentence in *Northanger Abbey* about the " three duodecimo volumes, two hundred and seventy-six pages in each, with a frontispiece to the first of two tombstones and a lantern." Both in literature and in art it was the engraftment upon the native *goût du sombre* of that " sensibility " which had become dominant over popular taste. In its specific sense, that word seems to come into use about the middle of the century ; it is found as a full-blown dogma in the *Sentimental Journey* (1768), which, together with *The Man of Feeling* (1771), was an established classic for the whole of the next generation.

But it was not into France alone that Young's fame extended. France dictated the laws of taste to Europe ; and the *Night Thoughts* were translated into Spanish, Italian, German, Portuguese, Swedish, and even Magyar. Klopstock, as might be expected, was besotted with them, and there is a letter extant from Frau Klopstock to Richardson in 1758, in which that worthy woman expresses surprise and pain that any one but Young should be thought of to fill the then vacant See of Canterbury.

Such an elevation for him was indeed far beyond the dreams of Young himself or of any rational being. But he had friends who would willingly have made him a bishop, just as the Duchess of Portland had a scheme, after he was left a widower, of marrying him to Mrs.

Pendarves—better known by her later name of Mrs.
Delany—and worried him a good deal over it, with no
result.   The reputation which grew up about Young of
his being a time-server and a place-seeker was brought on
him largely by the ill-advised pressure of his friends and
some weakness of his own in yielding to them.

He seems never to have defended himself against these
or other accusations, which were, indeed, mostly brought
forward after his death.   The story, long current, of the
Lorenzo of the *Night Thoughts*, a lay-figure meant to
represent a finished atheist and profligate, having been
drawn by him from his own son, is disposed of by the
simple fact that his son was at the time a boy of seven.
The scandal about his last years and his relations with his
housekeeper was equally baseless.   When he did make
suit for place or promotion, he seems always to have done
so like a man pushed on from behind, ungracefully,
reluctantly, and half-heartedly ; this is most striking in
his famous letter to Lady Suffolk, *maîtresse en titre* and
chief dispenser of Court patronage to George II, of which
so much has been made.   Indeed, he owed but little in
life either to his own solicitations or to those of others for
him.   A Civil List pension of £200 a year was no unreasonable recognition of one who at the time it was given
had no secured means of livelihood, and who had attained,
in poetry and in the drama, high reputation as a man of
letters.   The Clerkship of the Closet to the Dowager
Princess of Wales, given him after the accession of George
III when he was nearly eighty years old, was a slight and
belated compliment to an outworn patriarch.   He has
been roundly accused of taking orders for the sake of
emolument.   That he took this step in mature life—he
was then forty-four—appears to be the only basis for such
a suggestion ; and it is totally irrelevant.   Nothing in his

life, either before or after, suggests any motives for taking orders which were not sincere and honourable. Addison had thoughts of doing the same, but never could quite make up his mind to do it. It may be noted in passing, that Young's marriage to Lady Elizabeth Lee, like Addison's to the Countess of Warwick, was one of affection based on mutual esteem. His sole ecclesiastical preferment was the Rectory of Welwyn, to which he was presented by his own College, which he held till his death, and the duties of which he fulfilled without reproach.

But a certain unluckiness pursued him through life. As one of the " wits " in his youth he belonged to that group of very minor Oxford luminaries whose absurd names, hitched into a Latin verse, became a byword and a source of inextinguishable amusement—Tickell, Crabb and Trapp, Bubb and Grubb and Stubb. His fine, and in the phrase of the period, " sublime " poem of *The Last Day*—it is as good technically, Johnson justly remarks, as anything he ever wrote—missed its mark as regards any reward he may have coveted by being dedicated to Queen Anne just a month or so before her death. The persons of eminence to whom he inscribed the successive instalments of the *Night Thoughts* had none of them, except the Duchess of Portland, any interest in literature, and any more interest in morality or religion than became people of their quality. At his death, all his correspondence, including that with Addison and Swift, and later, with Richardson, was destroyed by his executors. " A polite hermit and a witty saint," as Mrs. Montagu called him, he half sought and half shrunk from prominence, and was hampered by his integrity in getting much profit out of his wit and worldliness. His father retained his College Fellowship for years by fraudulent concealment of the marriage by which he had

forfeited it. Such lapses were not uncommon, and seem
to have been regarded as venial obliquities. At all events,
it did not stand in the way of his becoming Dean of
Salisbury. The son would have been incapable of such
an action, and lived and died a mere country parson ;
from which Swift might have drawn the lesson, either that
the sins of the fathers are visited on the children, or that
we may gather what the Almighty thinks of Deaneries by
regarding those on whom He has thought fit to bestow
them.

The verse which Young inscribed on the alcove in his
garden at Welwyn, *Ambulantes in horto audiverunt vocem
Dei*, was, we may reasonably believe, not a mere piece of
cleverness, but a truth sincerely felt, and felt the more
after the passing of the Augustans had left him a solitary
figure in a new generation. If he wrote, as Johnson
truly remarks, " with very little operation of judgment,"
if he often provokes the same great critic's scornful comment " let burlesque try to go beyond him ! " on the
gaucheries which deform so much of his work, what
Horace Walpole says is also true, that " even in his most
frantic rhapsodies there are innumerable fine things."
When all is said, he had genius ; he was a poet ; and
that spent fame is not quite extinct, but still smoulders
faintly under its ashes.

COLLINS, AND THE ENGLISH LYRIC IN THE EIGHTEENTH CENTURY

A LECTURE GIVEN AT THE ROYAL SOCIETY OF
LITERATURE, 21 JANUARY 1920

COLLINS, AND THE ENGLISH LYRIC
IN THE EIGHTEENTH CENTURY

By common consent it is in the sphere of the lyric that English poetry has throughout its history found its fullest, highest, and, one might say, most authentic expression. We possess a body of lyrical poetry to which, alike in range and in beauty, that of Greece alone is comparable. It extends in an all but continuous chain, gathering itself at intervals into a blazing mass of jewels, over the last six centuries. The lyrical voice is our native and natural speech. The lyrical note pervades nearly all our greatest poetry, even when that embodies itself in other forms. At the periods when the lyrical impulse has flagged, when its expression has become for a time forced or languid, the life-blood of our poetry in general has been slower ; and our great lyric periods have been followed by a fresh impulse communicated from them into narrative or dramatic, descriptive or reflective poetry.

The eighteenth century—taking that convenient term in its broadly descriptive meaning and not as a strict chronological limit—is traditionally regarded as a period in which the lyric voice of poetry was feeble or almost dumb. This view requires much qualification. But it is substantially true for nearly the first half of the century. In the course of the seventeenth century enormous over-production had resulted in something like exhaustion. Our lyrical poetry became an unweeded garden, possessed more and more by things rank and gross in nature. It went astray in various directions ; it became tortuous or mystical or artificial. The lyric lost touch with Nature and life, and in doing so put off its own nature and lost its own enduring vitality. The immense popularity of Cowley lasted for a generation after his death ; but only a few years later, Pope's question, " Who now reads Cowley ? " could be asked. Cowley was, as Johnson says of him, " the last of the race " ; " the last," he repeats, and adds more doubtfully, " and perhaps the best." He only outlived by three years Herrick, who may share with Fanshawe the claim to be the last of the Elizabethans, and Milton, that lonely figure who spans the gulf that lies, with its swarming and confused poetic movement, between the Elizabethan and the Augustan age. Meanwhile, the civilisation of our poetry was being taken in hand. Its entry into the general European Commonwealth of letters was effected, but at a great cost. Between its own decay of over-ripeness and the desperate remedies which were applied, it lost much of its distinctive national quality. The English lyric soon, say by the death of Dryden on May Day in the last year of the century, became faint, mannered and almost voiceless. For a whole generation there is no English lyrical poet of the first or even of the second rank. What little vitality remained evident in the native instinct toward lyric expression was confined to a trickle of inspiration in the hymn-writers. Watts, Doddridge, Tate (who was Poet Laureate throughout the reign of Anne as well as being one of Pope's dunces), are followed a little later by John and Charles Wesley, the first collection of whose hymns was published in 1737. These are the more prominent figures in the chain of stepping-stones across a level and almost featureless marsh. The lighter and livelier verse of Prior and those of his contemporaries who wrote in the same manner, if it would be going too far to say that it can only be called poetry by courtesy, is hardly lyrical poetry except in a purely formal sense of the term.

But the lyrical instinct was not dead ; though it had been driven for a time below the surface, its springs were flowing underground ; it was waiting its time. The attempt to find any organic connection between political and poetical history, though enticing, is probably futile ; but it is a curious fact that the resurgence of the lyric first shows itself just after the collapse in 1742 of the long rule of Walpole. It was in that year that Gray wrote his Eton Ode and his *Hymn to Adversity*, and began to compose his *Elegy*. It was in that year that Collins came before the world with the Persian (afterwards re-named the Oriental) Eclogues. It is in that year that the re-emergence of the lyric in England may be definitely fixed, in so far as definite dates can be usefully assigned to the stages of what is a continuous vital process.

The re-emergence of romance had then already begun. It was initiated in Scotland by the publication eighteen years earlier of Allan Ramsay's *Evergreen*. The immediate and immense popularity of that collection showed that the thirst for romance was all the keener for having been temporarily stifled. Thomson brought the movement down into England. His *Seasons*, by far the most popular poetical work of their age, while they are in a mixed manner, won their success more by their romantic than by their classical element, though it was not until later, after the appearance of Collins' Odes and the earliest published of Gray's, that he made his decisive

mark as a romantic poet in the *Castle of Indolence*.   But
in 1742 the romantic movement was effectively launched.
Its progress thereafter may be traced from point to point,
like that of the successive waves of a swiftly-rising tide,
through the two Wartons—Joseph Warton's Odes, in
their own measure an epoch-making volume, were
published almost simultaneously with those of Collins—
Macpherson's *Ossian* (1742), Percy's *Reliques* (1765),
Chatterton (1768), Cowper's first substantial volume
of poems (1782), Blake's *Poetical Sketches* (1785), Burns'
Kilmarnock volume (1786), Scott's *Lenore* (1796), and
the full splendour of the new day in the *Lyrical Ballads*
of 1798.   The movement is both steady and continuous,
and it covers, as will be seen from the dates just cited,
the larger part—say nearly two-thirds—of the eighteenth
century.   In poetry, as in other fields of human development, that century was in truth, after the pause and recoil
of its earlier years, the great germinal and constructive
age of the modern world.   The nineteenth century built,
largely and prodigally, on the foundations it had laid.
Of the task and the achievement of the twentieth it is still
too early to give an account or even to hazard a forecast.

This is to some extent a digression from the subject
indicated by the title of this study.   For there is no
necessary connection between the romantic movement
and the lyrical impulse.   Romance takes other forms
than lyrical, and many of the greatest triumphs of the
lyric are purely classical.   But the digression was almost
necessary in order to set the subject in its national and
historical perspective.   We may now return, with some
added clearness of view, to the consideration of Collins
and his poems.

There is perhaps no one else who takes a place in the
foremost rank of our poets on so slender a volume of

production. Collins died at the age of thirty-six. But the melancholia which had begun to prey upon him some eight years before his death developed rapidly into actual insanity, at first intermittent and then total. For effective purposes his life can hardly be reckoned much longer than that of Keats. Even so, a good deal of it is a blank as regards poetry. He was of unusual precocity, as is shown by the few extant fragments of what he wrote when he was a schoolboy at Winchester. But while he wrote easily and fluently, he wrote very intermittently ; and he is said to have destroyed most of what he wrote almost as soon as it was written. In the years after he came to London from Oxford he took to the life of a young man about town, lost the habit of concentration, and alternated fitful study with trivial though not scandalous dissipation. It may not be wholly fanciful to trace in him as in other Sussex poets a strain having some connection with their native air and soil : a certain *mollities* in both senses of that word, an exquisite delicacy and sensitiveness on the one hand and some weakness or lack of fibre on the other. Otway, the tenderest poet of his time (between whose life and that of Collins there are some striking resemblances), died in misery and broken-hearted at thirty-six. Hurdis, a shy and delicate genius, now almost forgotten, faded out of life at thirty-seven. They and Collins are the three principal names associated with Sussex in the annals of our poetry until quite modern times. It is right that the monument to Collins should be where it is—in Chichester Cathedral and not in Westminster Abbey. But one could wish that the verses inscribed on it had been by a finer hand than that of Hayley, another Sussex poet—if one may extend that name to him for the sake of a once great success and popularity—who is remembered now as the friend of

Blake and Cowper, but has otherwise long been a spent fame.

The scanty records of Collins' life show that he was a born romanticist, that even in boyhood he was an explorer or re-discoverer, and had read largely and appreciatively in that older literature which was then still in general eclipse. With more strength of character and greater vitality, and inspired by a finer genius, he might have done work in the history and criticism of English poetry comparable to that of his friend and schoolfellow Thomas Warton. A curious passage in Warton's "History of English Poetry" informs us of Collins' early researches into the then unmapped tract of the Elizabethan drama. Collins, who, he says, " had searched this subject with no less fidelity than judgment and industry," told him that the plot of Shakespeare's *Tempest* was taken from the Italian or Spanish romance of "Aurelio and Isabella." This attribution is erroneous. Warton supposes that Collins' memory had then failed " in his last calamitous indisposition," and that he had given him a wrong name. It seems probable that he had come across and read the actual source, Antonio de Eslava's *Noches de Invierno,* while engaged on his project of a history of the revival of learning. For this work he had made considerable collections. Warton was informed, " on undoubted authority," that he had finished the preliminary dissertation for his history, and that it was written with great judgment, precision and knowledge of the subject. But on his death it and all his papers were destroyed in a fit of angry petulance by his sister, Mrs. Sempill, in whose care, such as it was, his last melancholy years were spent. Beyond the slender volume of his poems and a single letter, nothing of his work survives ; nor is much added to these by the few records or notices made of him by his friends.

The poems of Collins can be enumerated in a few lines. They consist of the four Persian Eclogues of 1742 ; the twelve *Odes on Several Descriptive and Allegoric Subjects* of 1747 ; two short and graceful pieces written at Winchester in 1739 ; the commendatory verses on Hanmer's Shakespeare of 1743—a piece of commonplace hack-work which ought to have died stillborn, and the reprinting of which among Collins' poems, though perhaps necessary, is an unfortunate necessity ; the famous *Ode on the Death of Thomson*, in 1747, written at the time, and printed in the next year, and the no less famous *Dirge in Cymbeline* of about the same date ; and the incomplete *Ode on the Popular Superstitions of the Highlands of Scotland*, given by him in MS. to Home in 1749, but printed for the first time forty years later in the *Transactions of the Royal Society of Edinburgh*.

To these pieces must be added one more—the interesting and characteristic verses " written on a paper which contained a piece of Bride-Cake given to the Author by a Lady." It offers a curious analogy to Gray's Stanzas to Mr. Bentley. Each contains a single stanza in the author's finest manner ; and a comparison of their technical evolution and of their cadences and phrasing (both being in the same metre, the elegiac quatrain) give a good criterion of the kindred yet very distinct gift of the two poets : the more so, that the remaining stanzas in both pieces are uninspired and commonplace, and neither are nor profess to be poetry in any high sense. Here is Gray's :

> But not to one in this benighted age
> Is that diviner inspiration given
> That burns in Shakespeare's or in Milton's page,
> The pomp and prodigality of heaven.

And here Collins' :

Ambiguous looks that scorn and yet relent,
Denials mild, and firm unaltered truth,
Reluctant pride and amorous faint consent,
And meeting ardours and exulting youth.

It was by his Eclogues that Collins won such fame as he attained in his lifetime. They are remarkable, not merely as the work of a boy of twenty or twenty-one, but as the revelation of a new voice in poetry. That he had already mastered the management of the couplet was but a little thing, for that was already becoming, what Cowper called it later, " a mere mechanic art." What gives the Eclogues their value is the appearance, in so artificial a medium as the pastoral, of an unequalled limpidity and a delicate sweetness. These qualities foreshadow the greater triumph of the Odes. The new voice has made itself audible, though it is still uncertain. In the middle of a passage of correct but quite conventional versification:

Here make thy Court amidst our rural scene
And shepherd girls shall own thee for their queen.
With thee be Chastity, of all afraid,
Distrusting all, a wise suspicious maid.
No wild desires amidst thy train be known,
But Faith, whose heart is fixed on one alone,
Desponding Meekness with her downcast eyes,
And friendly Pity, full of tender sighs—

one comes, with a shock of amazed delight, on the line,

Cold is her breast, like flowers that drink the dew.

Again, in the couplet,

Here, where no springs in murmurs break away
Or moss-crowned fountains mitigate the day,

the notes are within the compass, and closely resemble the manner, of Pope's earlier poetry. But in this other from the same Eclogue,

Oft to the shades and low-roofed cots retired
Or sought the vale where first his heart was fired,

there is a sensitiveness and a melodiousness such as, except by Goldsmith, is hardly reached again for the next fifty years. And similarly, one must await Wordsworth for a feeling for Nature so true and so fine (though the diction remains Augustan) as there is in—

What time the moon had hung her lamp on high
And passed in radiance through the cloudless sky.

The twelve Odes of 1747 contain Collins' central lyric achievement. But the little shilling volume in which they appeared fell dead. Of the one thousand copies printed, hardly any were sold. When, a year later, Collins inherited some £2000 from an uncle, the first use he made of the money was to buy up and burn the remainder. They were not reprinted until twenty years later, when their author had long been dead.

One of the few purchasers of the luckless volume was Gray. His criticism on it, in a letter to Warton, is very curious. The young author, he writes, is " the half of a considerable man " : he has " a fine fancy, modelled upon the antique, a bad ear, great variety of words, and images with no choice at all." All Gray's criticisms deserve and repay careful study. But this one is startling in its apparent want of appreciation. It seems as if he had written hastily, after a perfunctory and possibly a jealous glance at the Odes. This may be said in his justification, that the contents of the volume are very unequal, and some are of inferior merit. The Ode to Fear, after the magnificent opening couplet :

Thou, to whom the world unknown
With all its shadowy shapes is shown,

drags and trails, and here and there in it the reproach of

L

a bad ear is deserved. The Ode to Liberty ends in a huddle of images. The short Odes to Mercy and to Peace are undistinguished and even mechanical. A still lower level is reached in the Ode on the Death of Colonel Ross. But that was written to order, or at all events not spontaneously. Its interest lies in the fact that it is the raw material of what he distilled and crystallised into the matchless " How sleep the brave." For these two divine stanzas praise would be an impertinence. They are almost too familiar to quote, yet I cannot deny myself the delight of quoting them, to linger once more over their exquisite clarity and unequalled melodiousness. By a further stroke of genius, Collins gave them no title ; they are merely headed " Ode written in the beginning of the year 1746."

> How sleep the Brave, who sink to Rest
> By all their Country's Wishes blest !
> When *Spring*, with dewy Fingers cold,
> Returns to deck their hallow'd Mold,
> She there shall dress a sweeter Sod
> Than *Fancy's* Feet have ever trod.
>
> By Fairy Hands their Knell is rung,
> By Forms unseen their Dirge is sung ;
> There *Honour* comes, a Pilgrim grey,
> To bless the Turf that wraps their Clay,
> And *Freedom* shall a-while repair,
> To dwell a weeping Hermit there ! [1]

That is neither classical nor romantic ; the word " style " hardly applies to it, for it transcends style. It is simply and wholly right.

Now, the thought of the last four lines is thus put in the *Ode on the Death of Colonel Ross in the Action of Fontenoy*. Fontenoy was fought on May 11, 1745, and

---

[1] The original typography is here reproduced.

the Ode probably written soon after the arrival of the news. Both Odes were first published, together, in Dodsley's "Museum" early in 1746.

Blest youth, regardful of thy doom,
Aërial hands shall build thy tomb,
   With shadowy trophies crown'd ;
Whilst Honour bath'd in tears shall rove
To sigh thy name thro' every grove,
   And call his heroes round.

.   .   .   .

But lo, where sunk in deep despair,
Her garments torn, her bosom bare,
   Impatient Freedom lies !
Her matted tresses madly spread,
To every sod, which wraps the dead,
   She turns her joyless eyes.

To place the two stanzas and the two couplets into which they were transfigured beside each other and consider them is a lesson in the art of poetry. It would be strange that Collins let both pieces have a place in his volume of Odes but for the personal reasons which made him unwilling to suppress the former. The lady to whom it was addressed had been affianced to Colonel Ross, and Collins himself was her rejected lover. As originally printed, the first of the two stanzas I have cited was even feebler. It ran :

O'er him whose doom thy virtues grieve
Aërial forms shall sit at eve,
   And bend the pensive head !
And, fall'n to save his injur'd land,
Imperial Honour's awful hand
   Shall point his lonely bed !

This is artificial, commonplace, and even barely grammatical. But the whole sixty lines of the ode are hopelessly mannered, and the manner is hopelessly bad. If it were the first that Gray's eye lighted on, one can quite understand how it should have prejudiced him against the whole volume.

But on the very next page comes the immortal *Ode to Evening*. Of it little need be said; it is beyond criticism. It has a secure and unquestioned place in the very front rank of English lyrics. The unrhymed stanza in which it is written he took from Milton's celebrated experiment, the translation of the Fifth Ode of the First Book of Horace's Odes. As a metrical device the two pieces stand wholly by themselves. None of the few later attempts in the same form—for instance, Joseph Warton's graceful but undistinguished rendering of the Horatian Ode to the Spring of Bandusia (1776)—are of any consequence. But the two are only the same in their formal metrical structure. The rhythm and phrasing of Milton's piece are all his own ; he conveyed into it his unique and inimitable organ-tone. But Collins' ode is an equal feat of skill and genius, as inimitable in its delicacy and limpid clarity, like that of exquisite flute-music.

It seems to have passed over the heads of his contemporaries. The only one of the twelve Odes which became widely popular was the last, *The Passions : An Ode for Music*. This is in effect a new essay in the manner of Dryden's *St. Cecilia* Ode, and it therefore came on its readers with no strangeness ; they were, as one might say, already educated for it. Langhorne, who represents the prevalent standard of criticism of his time, a generation after Collins' death, speaks of it with unbounded and indeed extravagant praise. " It contains," he says, " the whole soul and power of poetry," and " there may be very little hazard," he adds, "in asserting that this is the finest ode in the English language." In itself, though its excellence admits of no question, it is not Collins at his highest ; it is, as has been well said of it, " a work of less equal sustentation and purity of excellence than the *Ode to Evening*," though the relative inferiority still leaves it in a high place.

Collins' delicacy and purity of taste had in them, as we have seen, an element of weakness ; he had not the architectural genius or the driving power for sustained workmanship. That " solitary song-bird," though he seldom makes a false note, has a limited compass. In the unfinished *Ode on the Popular Superstitions of the Highlands*, which is much the longest of his poems, one feels him working to a scale a little beyond his compass. The note is still pure and clear, but it is appreciably weakened.

From their own time till now, Collins and Gray have invited and almost compelled comparison. Their names are linked as the two great lyrical poets of their age, with no name to set beside or even next to them. They are strict contemporaries. Gray, though he outlived Collins by fifteen years, was born only five years before him. Both were fine scholars, though the scholarship of Gray was superior both in extent and in accuracy to that of Collins, as to that of any other Englishman of his time. The poetical product of both was small and exquisite. Gray's Odes, on the most liberal computation, only amount in all to some eight hundred lines, Collins' to about a thousand. Gray's output was small from his extraordinary fastidiousness and low vitality ; Collins' rather from lack of concentration, and a febrile temperament which he had not strength to keep in control. Which of the two had the finer poetical genius is a question which has been much debated, but which it is idle to pursue. The distinction, not the comparison between them, is what is important. As to this, the well-known dictum

of Swinburne may be taken as the starting-point : " As
an elegiac poet," he says, " Gray holds for all ages to
come his unassailable and sovereign station ; as a lyric
poet, he is simply unworthy to sit at the feet of Collins."

This saying, expressed as it is with Swinburne's usual
vehemence of exaggeration, contains a truth ; but it
requires scrutiny and large qualification.   In the first
place, the terms " lyric " and " elegiac " require to be
defined if we are to keep clear of confusion.   In their
popular use they involve a cross-division.   Technically
the lyric in any poetry is a strophic form, meant to be,
or capable of being, set to music and sung in verses.
Technically the elegiac is simply one form of the lyric,
written in couplets of a particular metrical construction.
But from its specialised use for poems on the dead, it
gradually acquired its modern sense, under which it is
practically equivalent to the Greek threnody.   Already
when it passed from Greek to Latin it had become the
flebilis elegeia of the Augustan poets.   Nowadays it is used
loosely and vaguely to describe reflective poetry of a grave
and serious, though not necessarily of a melancholy tone.
It is clear therefore that the elegy may be, and it often is,
merely one particular variety of the ode.   Both names
are often used indifferently of the same poem.   Gray's
Elegy—a fact generally forgotten—is so named in virtue
of the last three stanzas, the epitaph with which the piece
concludes.   Dryden's poem " to the pious memory of
Mrs. Anne Killigrew " was entitled by him an ode, but
is generally, and reasonably, classed among elegies.
Collins' own two lovely poems, most characteristic in his
peculiar excellence, and equal to his very best, " In
yonder grave a Druid lies," and " To fair Fidele's grassy
tomb," are both elegiac ; but the former was entitled
by him an ode, and the latter a dirge.   What

Swinburne's criticism seems to imply is, first, that Gray's poetical sovereignty rests on his *Elegy*—which as a matter of historical fact and of the *communis sensus generis humani* is true—and further, that apart from it, his body of Odes, that is to say his other lyric poetry, is of inferior rank to that of Collins. On a question of this kind opinions will always differ, as they always must differ when the attempt is made to weigh one kind of poetry in the scales against another kind of poetry. For the lyric in its full sense covers a vast field, in which there is room for kinds which are so disparate as to be properly not comparable.

While Gray owes his universal popularity to his *Elegy*, it was not what he desired his fame to rest upon. It would have been as popular, he said of it himself with a touch of bitterness, if it had been written in prose. In truth this is its unique value—that it embodies, in fault-less and imperishable verse, thoughts and emotions which are universal and eternal. But his odes are likewise, in the full sense, classic. They have their faults ; the minute laboriousness of workmanship is sometimes too evident, the inspiration sometimes flags. There are even passages which give colour to the accusation that has been (most exaggeratedly) made against him of " fanfaronade and falsetto." From these faults at least the easier and more spontaneous lyric of Collins is always free. He may be, he is sometimes, commonplace, but he is never strained. His wonderful clarity never deserts him. It is a flowing spring, not drops wrung out. His greatest felicities always seem his most spontaneous utterances. While he wrote in the style of his own age, he trans-muted it into something individual ; and so he is the least mannered, not only among the poets of his time, but almost in the whole body of our poetry. Language in his hands becomes absolutely or all but absolutely translucent.

Even his return upon the vocabulary of the older poets, though he occasionally indulges in it a little more, perhaps, than one could wish, never passes into pedantry or artificiality. In the *Ode to Evening* there is only one single word, *brede*—" with brede ethereal wove "—of which we cannot say that it is not merely the right word, but once it is there, apparently the most straightforward and most inevitable. Perhaps the one thing that can be called a mannerism in him is his fondness for compound epithets ; *young-eyed* and *chaste-eyed* ; *sky-born* and (less happily) *sky-worn* ; *fancy-blest, soul-subduing, war-denouncing, rich-haired, green-haired, bright-haired, light-embroidered* and *sphere-descended* ; and, used by him twice with triumphant beauty, *dim-discovered*. Here Collins followed the example set and popularised by Thomson in *The Seasons*. But his tact in the use of the device, unlike that of Thomson, who overdoes it, is nearly faultless ; *sphere-found* and *scene-full* are perhaps his only two failures. To have gained this enrichment without impairment of clarity is one of his wonderful achievements.

I am not sure whether it has ever been noticed that in the celebrated vindicatory preface by John Wesley to the collection of his own and his brother's hymns, there is what seems to be an oblique censure on Collins in this matter. " By labour," Wesley writes, " a man may become a tolerable imitator of Spenser, Shakespeare or Milton ; and may heap together many pretty compound epithets, as *pale-eyed, meek-eyed,* and the like ; but unless he be born a poet, he will never attain the genuine spirit of poetry." *Pale-eyed* and *meek-eyed*, it will be remembered, both occur in Milton's *Nativity Ode*, and they no doubt suggested, or helped to suggest, Collins' similar formations, though, of course, *young-eyed* was taken by

him straight from Shakespeare. Only, Collins happened
to be born a poet.

Even in his inferior odes, Collins often reaches, by
instinct and seemingly without effort, to his incomparable
translucency. Thus, for instance, in the *Ode on the
Poetical Character* :

> When He, who called with thought to birth
> Yon tented sky, this laughing earth,
> And dressed with springs and forests tall,
> And poured the main engirting all.

Thus in the *Ode to Liberty* :

> Beyond yon braided clouds that lie
> Paving the light-embroidered sky.

The " return to Nature," of which he was one of the
prime initiators, expresses itself in phrases to which
Arnold, a century later, offers the nearest parallel.
" Teach me but once like him to feel," Collins writes of
Shakespeare ; the cry is that of Arnold's *Memorial
Verses on the Death of Wordsworth*, " But who, ah !
who will make us feel ? " In the noble *Ode to Simplicity*,
the eighth stanza sums up what may be called Collins'
poetical doctrine or his poetical message, though both
these terms are open to exception :

> Though taste, though genius bless
> To some divine excess,
> Faints the cold work till thou inspire the whole ;
> What each, what all supply
> May court, may charm our eye,
> Thou, only thou, canst raise the meeting soul !

Of Collins, as of some other poets, notably of Coleridge
—to whom Collins presents some curious and fertile
analogies—it is to be observed that their finest and most
characteristic work is wholly unique. Where it can be

brought into comparison with that of other poets of the first rank it is apt to be inferior to theirs. It would be tempting to pursue this point somewhat into detail, but would lead us too far from the main subject at present. One pair of instances may suffice to indicate what I mean. When Collins writes in the *Ode on Popular Superstitions*,

> For him in vain his anxious wife shall wait
> Or wander forth to meet him on his way ;
> For him in vain at to-fall of the day
> His babes shall linger at the unclosing gate,[1]

one is inevitably reminded of the stanza in Gray's *Elegy*, written at almost exactly the same time :

> For them no more the blazing hearth shall burn
> Or busy housewife ply her evening care,
> No children run to lisp their sire's return,
> Or climb his knees the envied kiss to share.

Collins' lines have, even here, his wonderful limpid quality, and his felicity in the avoidance of merely ornamental or otiose epithet. Note, too, the particularity (a note of the lyric) in contrast with Gray's superb generalisation. But Gray's touch is stronger, his music richer and ampler. The contrast of the two quatrains gives the key to the distinction between Gray and Collins as lyrists.

Similarly, when reading in Coleridge's *Ode to Sara*,

> The tears that tremble down your cheek
> Shall bathe my kisses chaste and meek
>   In pity's dew divine ;
> And from your heart the sighs that steal
> Shall make your rising bosom feel
>   The answering swell of mine :

one's mind passes at once to Wordsworth's—

---

[1] He had written " at the cottage gate " first.

And vital feelings of delight
Shall rear her form to stately height,
  Her virgin bosom swell ;
Such thoughts to Lucy I will give
While she and I together live
  Here in this happy dell :

and beside it, Coleridge's lines, with all their melodious
ease, lose their lustre, and faint like a dazzled morning
moon.

The poetical affinity between Collins and Coleridge at
which I have hinted has, I think, largely escaped notice.
It would repay study. Even the circumstances of their
life, as well as their peculiarities of mental temperament,
present curious analogies. Both had, and doubtless had
to pay for, a remarkable precocity of genius. Both
suffered from languor of mood and infirmity of will.
Both wrote with seemingly effortless ease, and with
fluctuating inspiration. The poetical production of both,
or what matters of it, is confined within a space of five or
six years, followed in the one by mental collapse and early
death, in the other, by that joyless atrophy of which
Coleridge himself in his swan-song, the Dejection Ode,
has given the perfect and immortal account.

In one of Coleridge's early pieces, written in 1793—
or so he says, and in this instance there seems no reason
to believe that he is not telling the truth—there is a
passage which, if it were now to be published for the first
time as a recovered fragment by Collins, would probably
be accepted as his without question ; for the style,
rhythm and diction are in all respects indistinguishable
from his :

For lo ! attendant on thy steps are seen
Graceful Ease in artless stole
And white-robed Purity of soul,
With Honour's softer mien ;

Mirth of the loosely flowing hair,
And meek-eyed Pity eloquently fair,
Whose tearful cheeks are lovely to the view,
As snowdrop wet with dew.

Had Collins, at the critical period (described with such just insight and sympathetic understanding by Johnson) when he was adrift as a young man in London, come into contact with a complementary genius, as Coleridge did with that of Wordsworth, it is difficult to set limits to the poetical splendours which might have resulted. But that is a vain speculation. As it was, he had no one but the two Wartons, whose outlook was in effect the same as his own, and who in any case were not made out of the material that strikes fire by contact. Had he known Gray, perhaps—— Yet even there the essential difference—one of pitch as well as of key—might only have produced an incurable discord.

As it is, the tiny volume of his poems places him imperishably in England's Helicon. It gives for perpetuity that image of which Wordsworth speaks in the lines headed *Remembrance of Collins*, composed, like the exquisite ode to which they refer, on the Thames near Richmond :

The image of a poet's heart,
How bright, how solemn, how serene !

Fame did not come to him in his life ; but it did not fail to overtake him later, and it will not leave him now.

THE COMPOSITION OF KEATS' "ENDYMION"

28 November 1920

THE COMPOSITION OF KEATS' "ENDYMION"

Enquiry into the circumstances and surroundings in which a great work of art was produced, if it be subject to obvious dangers and abuses, is always interesting, and may be useful. If it throw some fresh light on the work itself, if it quicken our appreciation, it can be vindicated from the charge of idle curiosity. As regards the composition of *Endymion*, there is little to add to the lucid and delightful account given by Sir Sidney Colvin in Chapter V of his "Life of Keats." But that account may be pursued into somewhat further detail ; and, in particular, we may find in the poem passages which bear, with probability if not with certainty, traces of their immediate occasion and origin. To do so is the purpose of this paper.

Keats did not write *Endymion* at random, improvising as he went on. Before he began it in April, 1817, he had planned out the scheme of its contents ; had determined that it should be in four books containing 4000 lines ; and had even allotted the time that would be required to write it. It is remarkable how closely he carried out his plan. "Let Autumn," he wrote in the lovely poem,

> With universal tinge of sober gold
> Be all about me when I make an end.

Late autumn was just passing into winter when he did so. Its actual composition occupied just over seven months ; and as finally published, after revision, in the following April, it contained 4048 lines.   Keats' movements during this period can be traced from his letters as follows.

On the evening of April 14th he travelled from London to Southampton by the night coach, and next day writes from there to his brothers that he is taking the boat to the Isle of Wight that afternoon.   On the 17th he writes to Reynolds that after having looked at Shanklin the day before, he has determined to settle down at Carisbrooke, where he has accordingly established himself in lodgings at Mrs. Cook's, New Village (midway between Carisbrooke and Newport).   " I shall forthwith," he adds, " begin my *Endymion*."   The date of his leaving the Isle of Wight for Margate is uncertain ; the references to it are loosely given, and not quite consistent with one another if literally pressed.   His first letters from Margate are to Hunt and Haydon, both dated May 10th, and the latter continued on the 11th.   In that to Hunt, he says that " in a week or so " he became upset, through sleeplessness and unwholesome food, in the Isle of Wight, " and set off pell-mell for Margate."   " I began my poem about a fortnight since, and have done some every day except travelling ones."   The " travelling ones " are presumably the two days which must have been taken up by the journey from Carisbrooke to Margate ; it may, of course, have taken up the greater part of three.   To Haydon he says incidentally, speaking of Mrs. Cook and her lodgings, " I was but there a week."   On the 16th, however, he writes to Taylor and Hessey, " I went day by day at my poem for a month, at the end of which time the other day I found my brain so overwrought that

I . . . was obliged to give up for a few days. . . . However, to-morrow I will begin my next month. This evening I go to Canterbury, having got tired of Margate." When these indications are pieced together, it is pretty clear that he in fact began *Endymion*, as he meant to do, in the Isle of Wight ; it is quite clear that he went on with it at Margate ; and when he moved from Margate to Canterbury, he had got a good way on with Book I, though he had come for the time to a standstill and writes (to Haydon), " So now I revoke my promise of finishing my poem by the autumn."

How long he stayed at Canterbury, and whether he went straight back from there to London (that is, to Hampstead, to which the brothers migrated from their Cheapside lodgings in the spring or early summer of this year), we do not know ; there is a gap in the extant correspondence from May 16th till the beginning of September. But during these three months and a half, and in all probability mainly at Hampstead, he finished Book I and wrote Book II. Then he went to Bailey at Oxford ; on September 5th he writes from there to Reynolds' sisters, evidently within a few days after his arrival ; and to his sister Fanny on the 10th, that " it is now a week that I disembarked from his Whipship's Coach the Defiance in this place." He stayed there for a month ; what he says in his letter of October 8th to Bailey from Hampstead shows that he had not left Oxford later than the 5th, and probably had left it on that day. In the course of that month he and Bailey made an excursion to Stratford-on-Avon ; otherwise Keats was steadily at work on Book III daily ; on the 21st he writes to Reynolds, " I am getting on famous with my third book—have written 800 lines thereof, and hope to finish it next week,"—and on the 28th to Haydon,

M

" within these last three weeks I have written 1000 lines, which are the third book of my poem." As it finally appeared it contains 1032 lines. He was then at Hampstead until November 22nd, when he went down to Burford Bridge, with " 500 lines wanting to finish *Endymion* " ; in a letter to Reynolds written on the evening of his arrival, he transcribes what are now lines 581–590 of Book IV and asks for his opinion on them. He finished and dated the last line of the poem at Burford Bridge on November 28th.

Keeping this chronological sketch in our minds as a chart, we may read *Endymion* with a fresh interest ; with minds made more alert and receptive by keeping on the look-out for traces of particular suggestion and inspiration ; and where we see, or think we see, these, with some added insight into the process of poetical creation, the way in which the scenes or objects presented to the poet's senses are assimilated and then transmuted by the specific poetical imagination. Even negative results here may have their value : it is, for instance, both interesting and significant that in Book III, written, as we have seen, entirely at Oxford, there is so far as I can see not a single line or phrase in which the influence of Oxford can be found. I shall return to this point in its proper place.

In the earlier part of Book I, something in the landscape and atmosphere, as well as more particular touches here and there, brings the Isle of Wight vividly to mind for any one who has wandered about it in spring. The lines (37–45) in the opening passage,

> Each pleasant scene
> Is growing fresh before me as the green
> Of our own vallies ; so I will begin
> Now while I cannot hear the city's din ;
> Now while the early budders are just new,
> And run in mazes of the youngest hue

> About old forests ; while the willow trails
> Its delicate amber ; and the dairy pails
> Bring home increase of milk . . .

are of course an express description ; Parkhurst Forest
still retained its oaks notwithstanding the heavy drain of
naval timber from it during the Napoleonic wars ; and
for the rest, we may compare the descriptive passages in
the once famous *Dairyman's Daughter* of 1809. Further
on we have the music (lines 117–121) which

> . . . gave
> Its airy swellings, with a gentle wave,
> To light-hung leaves, in smoothest echoes breaking
> Through copse-clad vallies,—ere their death, o'ertaking
> The surgy murmurs of the lonely sea.

" The passage in *Lear*—' do you not hear the sea ? '—
has haunted me intensely," he had written to Reynolds
on April 17th. In the same letter he says, " I have found
several delightful wood-alleys, and copses, and quick
freshes . . . the trench (of Carisbrook Castle) is over-
grown with the smoothest turf, and the walls with ivy
. . . we will read our verses in a delightful place I have
set my heart upon, near the castle." The place he had
set his heart upon seems to reappear in lines 79–88 :

> Paths there were many,
> Winding through palmy fern, and rushes fenny
> And ivy banks ; all leading pleasantly
> To a wide lawn, whence one could only see
> Stems thronging all around between the swell
> Of turf and slanting branches : who could tell
> The freshness of the space of heaven above,
> Edg'd round with dark tree tops ? through which a dove
> Would often beat its wings, and often too
> A little cloud would move across the blue.

Already on his way down to Southampton he had seen
and been thrilled by such a " pomp of dawn " and such

" glories of sunrise " as he describes in the lines immediately following these. "*N.B. this Tuesday Morn saw the Sun rise*—of which I shall say nothing at present. . . . From dawn till half-past six I went through a most delightful country, some open down, but for the most part thickly wooded. What surprised me most was an immense quantity of blooming furze on both sides the road." It reappears, perhaps (line 202), in the

> Swelling downs, where prickly furze
> Buds lavish gold.

And there seems a recollection, not at the time, but much further on in the poem, of his visit to Shanklin on April 16th—" a most beautiful place. Sloping wood and meadow ground reach round the Chine, which is a cleft . . . filled with trees and bushes in the narrow part, and as it widens out becomes bare, if it were not for primroses on one side, which spread to the very verge of the sea, and some fishermen's huts on the other, perched midway in the balustrades of beautiful green hedges along their steps down to the sands. But the sea—then the white cliff—then St. Catherine's Hill—the sheep in the meadows ! "—in II, 73,

> One track unseams
> A wooded cleft, and far away, the blue
> Of ocean fades upon him ;

and in Glaucus' description of his fisher-life, III, 357 foll.,

> I would steer
> My skiff along green shelving coasts, to hear
> The shepherd's pipe come clear from airy steep,
> Mingled with ceaseless bleatings of his sheep.
>   . . . Constantly
> At brim of day-tide, on some grassy lea
> My nets would be spread out.

In the *Hymn to Pan* (sung on an April morning, line 217)

the island landscape seems to reappear where one might not expect it ; not in the

> sunny meadows that outskirt the side
> Of thine enmossed realms,

so clearly as in

> The dreary melody of bedded reeds
> In desolate places, where dank moisture breeds
> The pipy hemlock to strange overgrowth,

and the

> undescribèd sounds
> That come a swooning over hollow grounds
> And wither drearily on barren moors,

which recall the melancholy and untenanted tract of marshy lowland known as the Wilderness about the upper waters of the Medina, haunted by wailing plover and by the distant sound of the sea beyond the downs.

Here or hereabouts, we should expect any local suggestion to pass from the Isle of Wight to Kent, where now (line 470) " the dew brings incense from the fields of May." There is but little of this obvious. What came before Keats' eyes at Margate may have left its influence in lines 529–530 :

> I, who still saw the horizontal sun
> Heave his broad shoulder o'er the edge of the world,

and at the beginning of Book II :

> Wide sea, that one continuous murmur breeds
> Along the pebbled shore of memory,
> Many old rotten-timbered boats there be
> Upon thy vaporous bosom, magnified
> To goodly vessels.

Nor is there any very certain trace of Canterbury ; though the effect of the Cathedral on the poet's imagination may

be surmised in several descriptions of the underground
realm which Endymion traverses in Book II :

> Dark nor light
> The region ; nor bright nor sombre wholly,
> But mingled up ; a gleaming melancholy ;
> A dusky empire and its diadems.
>
> (lines 221-224)
>
> Stepping awfully
> The youth approached ; oft turning his veil'd eye
> Down sidelong aisles, and into niches old.
> And when more near against the marble cold
> He had touched his forehead, he began to thread
> The courts and passages, where silence dead
> Rous'd by his whispering footsteps murmured faint.
>
> (lines 262-286)

and, more assuredly, in

> the wrought oaken beams,
> Pillars, and frieze, and high fantastic roof
> Of those dusk places in times far aloof
> Cathedrals call'd.
>
> (lines 623-626)

It would be delightful to identify the well, with auriculas
growing in the " gaps and slits " of its " slabbed margin,"
the minute picture of which (lines 869–880) looks like a
close transcript from nature ; but identification is probably impossible.

Book III, as we have seen, was wholly written at
Oxford. Neither in it, nor in any of Keats' letters from
Oxford, is there any sign that the romance and magic of
the city appealed to him : if they did, he must have shut
off, or reserved, the imaginative impression. One might
conjecture that he deliberately rebelled against this as
a disturbing influence ; much as, on his return from
Oxford to London, he refused Shelley's invitation to stay
with him at Marlow. There is an accent of petulance in

what he writes to Fanny : " This Oxford I have no doubt is the finest city in the world—it is full of old Gothic buildings, spires, towers, quadrangles, cloisters, groves, etc.," in their contrast of tone with the words that follow, " and is surrounded with more clear streams than ever I saw together. I take a walk by the side of one of them every evening." It reappears in the burlesque verses he sent to Reynolds, with their cheap witticisms on " the mouldering arch next door to Wilson the hosier," and the " plenty of trees, and plenty of fat deer for parsons " which is all that he has to say of Magdalen Grove. Perhaps in reaction against praise of Oxford with which he had been flooded before going, he takes or affects the attitude of a rather ill-bred revolutionary. A deeper impression might have developed later. For the profound effect of Canterbury upon him only appears two years after he had left it, in the *Eve of St. Mark*, and then under the reinforcing influence of his visit to Chichester and his long stay at Winchester.

The first half of Book IV was composed at Hampstead ; it is there no doubt that (lines 294–297) he

> listened to the wind that now did stir
> About the crisped oaks full drearily,
> Yet with as sweet a softness as might be
> Remembered from its velvet summer song,

and walked on the Heath when (lines 484–486)

> The good-night blush of eve was waning slow,
> And Vesper, risen star, began to throe
> In the dusk heavens silverly.

The passage about the Cave of Quietude immediately following suggests that he had just about this point fallen into the fit of depression, and almost of mental torpor, from which he wished to rally himself by going away to

Burford Bridge, " to change the scene, change the air, and give me a spur to wind up my poem." The success of the change was triumphant ; and as it draws towards its conclusion, *Endymion* reaches a higher point in speed and splendour and exquisite poise of verse than anything which Keats had written till then.

The surroundings, Box Hill and the Mole valley, have impressed themselves quite unmistakably here. On the very evening of his arrrival he writes to Reynolds, in fresh, even in buoyant spirits : " I like this place very much. There is hill and dale and a little river. I went up Box Hill this evening after the moon, came down, and wrote some lines." Were they these ?

> Where shall our dwelling be ?   Under the brow
> Of some steep mossy hill, where ivy dun
> Would hide us up, although spring leaves were none ;
> And where dark yew-trees, as we rustle through,
> Will drop their scarlet berry cups of dew.

It might be the next day, in the fine November weather, that he wrote (lines 678–681)—

> For by one step the blue sky should'st thou find,
> And by another, in deep dell below,
> See through the trees a little river go
> All in its midday gold and glimmering ;

and later, lines 763–769—

> The Carian
> No word return'd : both lovelorn, silent, wan,
> Into the valleys green together went.
> Far wandering, they were perforce content
> To sit beneath a fair lone beechen tree,
> Nor at each other gaz'd, but heavily
> Por'd on its hazle cirque of shedded leaves.

It must surely have been on one of these days that he watched

how shadows shifted
Until the poplar tops, in journey dreary,
Had reached the river's brim,

and that

then up he rose
And slowly as that very river flows,
Walked towards the temple grove with this lament :

(was the temple grove at Dorking or Mickleham ?)

Why such a golden eve ?   The breeze is sent
Careful and soft, that not a leaf may fall.
. . . Night will strew
On the damp grass myriads of lingering leaves.
. . . So he inwardly began
On things for which no wording can be found,
Deeper and deeper sinking, until drown'd
Beyond the reach of music : for the choir
Of Cynthia he heard not, though rough briar
Nor muffling thicket interpos'd to dull
The vesper hymn, far swollen, soft and full,
Through the dark pillars of those sylvan aisles.
(lines 924-928, 933-934, 961-968)

One who has been reading *Endymion* again now, just at
the time of the year when its last line was written, may
well feel afresh the thrill of awed admiration :

Peona went
Home through the gloomy wood in wonderment.

WILLIAM MORRIS

An Address delivered in the Town Hall, Birmingham, at the Annual Meeting of the National Home Reading Union, 28 October 1910

WILLIAM MORRIS

In choosing William Morris as the subject of an address to the National Home Reading Union, and to the citizens of Birmingham who are interested in the work of the Union and in sympathy with its objects, I have had regard to three things. In the first place, Morris is one of the great English poets, and an author, both in poetry and in prose, of writings which are great in every sense —large in amount and splendid in quality. Next, the writings of Morris from first to last, and in one way or another, bear closely on actual life. They give a view of life, and a stimulus towards living, such as is given by few others. In reading his work, we have before us the work of one of the greatest of English artists, and one to whom art meant the realisation of the value of life and the beauty of the world. Lastly, Birmingham, though he did not belong to it, is associated in more than one way with important periods of his career. I need hardly remind you of the group of young Birmingham men whose friendship he made at Oxford, and who with him became the famous Oxford Brotherhood. I need hardly speak of the most eminent of that group, Burne-Jones, who was born and brought up here, and who was, from the time they first met until Morris died, his closest friend and constant associate, in life and thought and work. The windows in St. Philip's Church, which are one of the glories of Birmingham, were made by Morris' workmen under his close supervision from Burne-Jones' designs. They are one of the finest examples anywhere to be found of the splendid results that can be got by the co-operation of genius and skill in artists who are in fellowship with one another, and who tell for more than double because they have a single mind and aim. In your Municipal Art Gallery there are more examples of the same co-operation and its effects. I may remind you, too, that it was here, nearly thirty-two years ago, that Morris, as President of the Birmingham Society of Arts, began the practice of giving public addresses on Art and Life. That lecture, " The Art of the People," is printed in the volume entitled *Hopes and Fears for Art.* It was his first lecture at Birmingham, but by no means his last. Among this audience there may be some who heard it. These lectures of his, many of which have now been collected and printed, still retain for their readers all their old stimulus and suggestion and value, although they cannot give on the pages of a book the full effect of his personality and presence.

To speak of Morris is in one way easy, because the matter is so abundant. His genius overflowed into almost every kind of human activity. It extended far beyond the boundaries of any single occupation or profession. In speaking to and on behalf of the National Home Reading Union, I shall deal with him, of course, primarily and mainly as an author whose works are to be read, and cannot be read too much. But he was more than a man of letters ; he was a great artist and craftsman, a great citizen, a great vital force for his own generation and for ours. And this in another way makes the task of speaking of him difficult, from the mere embarrassment of riches. Two things must be borne in mind. First, all great artists live, in some measure, a life apart, a life into which others cannot fully enter. This is so with the artist in one kind of art, the great poet or romance-writer, the great painter or musician. It is no less true when, as was the case with Morris, their productive and imaginative powers were not confined to particular limits, but were directed from many sides towards a common social end. For the art to which Morris applied his genius was art in its whole width and its highest meaning ; it was the art of human life.

Secondly, Morris and his work were one and indivisible. Neither can be understood without understanding the other ; and no part of his work can be fully appreciated apart from all the rest. For it was all the natural out-come of one large and manifold and yet very simple personality. To him, all the arts were threaded on one centre : he passed from one kind of art to another quite easily, because they were all different ways of getting at the same thing. His outlook on them, his handling of them, were central and therefore unimpeded and coherent. I am not here to speak of Morris as a crafts-man ; yet I may say this in passing, that one keeps coming back to his work in the decorative arts from other work that is more modern, more clever, more showy, with an ever fresh sense of its truth and soundness. I am not here to speak of Morris as a Socialist, and of the way in which he applied his sense of design to the social fabric. I am here to speak of him as a writer, and above all, as a poet. But all these things were in harmony ; all were simply the same Morris manifesting himself in different ways. If you find any one of them excellent, you may be sure that there is the same kind of excellence in them all.

This comprehensiveness is perhaps the highest of his

achievements ; or rather, it is the sum and substance of
all his achievement.   In a distracted age, given over to
specialisation and not seeing any clear aim before it, he
showed that it was still possible to see life, and to practise
life, as a whole.   When I go on to speak about Morris'
writings, I would beg you to bear in mind that they are
all, however much they differ from one another, the work
of a great artist and craftsman when he was working in
the specific art of literature, as at other times he would
be working at pattern-designing or at weaving or dyeing
or printing ; that poetry, and prose too, was for him one
of the arts which jointly and in fellowship with one
another constitute Art ; and that Art meant to him the
joy and beauty of life.

It follows that Morris' books, like the other things he
made—and he was always making something—were
part of his life, taking visible shape in words ; and we
shall read them with more enjoyment and keener appreciation if we know something of his life and realise how his
poems and prose writings spring naturally and as it were
inevitably out of it.   I do not intend to give any sketch
of his life now.   It is known, I hope, in its main outlines
at least, to many of you ; if not, it easily can be.   The
story of it is given fully in my biography.   For those to
whom that book is not easily accessible, or who wish to
read it in a more compact form, I may recommend a
little book which came out a couple of years ago and is
very good, and also very cheap—Mr. Holbrook Jackson's
William Morris in the Social Reformers series, price six-
pence in paper covers or a shilling in cloth binding.   It
will stimulate you to read more about Morris, and it will
put you on the right lines towards understanding him.
And now I will go on to speak of Morris' own writings.

Even here, on this limited ground, it is the same as I

said it was with regard to Morris as a whole : the task
is in a way easy because the material is so rich ; it is in
a way difficult just because of the superabundance of the
material. Much of his work I must pass unnoticed.
We shall do best to distinguish the main groups into
which his writings fall, and to say something about each.
In doing this it is simplest to adopt a roughly chronological order. Also I shall lay most stress on his poetry :
for while Morris, even if he had never written any poetry,
would still be an English author of importance and of
great value, it is as a poet that he takes his rank among
authors ; and he is an English poet of the first rank. He
is one of the six great Victorian poets, and not the least
among them. It is indeed in a prose writing, the *Dream
of John Ball*, that he reached what is perhaps the culminating point of his whole work ; and in his last years he
almost left off writing poetry, and poured out the series
of beautiful prose romances which cannot be neglected
in any account of his work as a writer, however brief.
But speaking generally, we shall do best on this occasion
to consider him as a poet, and only to touch on his prose
writings very slightly.

It will be useful, then, to bear in mind that Morris'
poetry, in its main substance, falls naturally into three
groups, corresponding to three successive periods in his
life. First, there is the period of early lyric and romance.
This is represented by his first published volume, *The
Defence of Guenevere and other Poems*, written between
1856 and 1858, in his last year at Oxford, and during the
year or two after he had left it and settled down in London.
Next, there is the period of romantic narrative, represented by *The Life and Death of Jason* and *The Earthly
Paradise*, written between 1866 and 1870, in the full
prime of his early manhood. Then there is the period

N

of epic represented by *Sigurd the Volsung*, which was published in 1876. *Poems by the Way*, a most delightful collection made by him in 1891, contains both early and late pieces : it includes some of his most beautiful short poems. If we were giving anything like a summary of his writings, we should have to add as much again. We should have to add the prose stories which appeared in *The Oxford and Cambridge Magazine* in 1856 ; the very remarkable dramatic poem called *Love is Enough* which he wrote between *The Earthly Paradise* and *Sigurd* ; the translations into English verse of Virgil's *Æneid* and Homer's *Odyssey* ; many other translations from old French and Icelandic ; several volumes of lectures and addresses ; the *Dream of John Ball*, of which I have already spoken ; and the whole long series of prose romances written in the last eight years of his life, beginning with *The House of the Wolfings*, and ending with *The Sundering Flood*, which he finished only a few weeks before his death : and even this would not be all. He never wrote anything that is not well worth reading ; and our admiration of his outstanding and central work in poetry is further quickened when we look at the immense mass and variety of his whole writings.

The Defence of Guenevere is a volume which the years have made more precious. It fell absolutely flat when it first appeared. It did not sell. The critics ignored it. It only began to become known when Morris ten years afterwards had won fame by his *Life and Death of Jason*. But on a small number of people then, and upon an increasingly greater number ever since, it produced a very deep effect ; and it is one of the books which are now recognised as having shaped the course and given a direction to the progress of English poetry. At the time when it appeared, the movement of poetry was at slack water between tides ; it was languid and uncertain. The most popular poets of the time were Longfellow, a poet whose work is indeed perfectly true and sound so far as it goes, but who can hardly be called a really great poet ; and Mrs. Browning, whose poetry was for the most part impassioned pamphleteering, and has not lasted. Just at that time Morris in this small and obscure volume gave the first voice to a new romantic revival. When I say the first voice, I do not of course forget that this revival had begun earlier, in the hands and through the genius of Rossetti. *The Blessed Damozel* had actually appeared in 1850. But Rossetti was not in any wide sense a figure among the English poets until he at last published his volume of *Poems* in 1870. And Morris, although this volume of his early poems owes much to Rossetti's influence, and is in fact inscribed to him in acknowledgment of that influence, had from the first, as he had all along, a genius which was wholly his own. His friend Dixon, one of the Birmingham members of the Oxford Brotherhood, described many years afterwards the effect produced on him by the very first poem that Morris ever wrote. " As he read it," he says, " I felt that it was something the like of which had never been heard before." So too Swinburne, the last of the six great Victorians, wrote of *The Defence of Guenevere* : " Upon no piece of work in the world was the impress of native character ever more distinctly stamped. This poet held of none, stole from none, clung to none, as tenant or as beggar or as thief." This judgment is completely just. These poems take up and carry forward the romantic movement in poetry from the point where Keats had dropped it at his death, and add to it a new touch of tragic passion, a new truth, and a new music. Pieces among them like *King Arthur's Tomb, The Eve of Crecy*,

Summer Dawn—I name three which are in completely different manners—are instances of romantic poetry in its full perfection of romanticism.   Morris was not yet a consummate artist, as he afterwards became ; he had not yet mastered the faculty of composition and design. But he was no pupil or beginner ; he was a living poet. There is still want of trained skill ; the voice is not yet under full control.   But it rings true, and is piercingly sweet.   Take as an example the brief lyric called *Summer Dawn.*

> Pray but one prayer for me 'twixt thy closed lips,
> Think but one thought of me up in the stars.
> The summer night waneth, the morning light slips
> Faint and grey 'twixt the leaves of the aspen, betwixt the cloud
>   bars
> That are patiently waiting there for the dawn,
> Patient and colourless, though heaven's gold
> Waits to float through them along with the sun.
> Far out in the meadows above the young corn
> The heavy elms wait, and restless and cold
> The uneasy wind rises ; the roses are dun ;
> Through the long twilight they pray for the dawn
> Round the lone house in the midst of the corn.
> Speak but one word to me over the corn,
> Over the tender, bowed locks of the corn.

That is the lovely dawn of poetry, waiting for the full daylight to come.   When he wrote the lines Morris was twenty-two.

Between *The Defence of Guenevere* and *The Life and Death of Jason* there are nine years : and in these years Morris had matured and made himself.   He had taken up and organised for himself the life of an artist.   Of the faculty of artistic design in its technical sense he had once for all showed himself a master in the decoration which he planned and executed at the Oxford Union in 1857.   He described himself in later years, when he had

to name his profession, as a designer. But design in its
larger sense, the designing of production, the designing
of life itself as a productive energy, was not only his
professional business, but in one form or another his
constant occupation, and his constant delight. He
carried it on with a perpetually widening range of application, and a perpetual deepening of the foundations
towards the bed-rock, towards principles which were
simple, final, and universal in their application. The
immediate occasion of his taking up this business in full
earnest was his marriage in 1859, and the house that he
then began to build for himself to live in. It became
quite clear, as this work went on, that in order to make
even a single house what it ought to be, the whole of the
industries connected with the building, decoration, and
furnishing of houses must be redesigned, must have fresh
life put into them. Now the house and the household,
with all that these words involve, were to Morris the
symbol and the embodiment of civilised human life.
Thus, in instinctive and yet reasoned adaptation to the
actual conditions of things, the poet became also a work-
man, and the Oxford Brotherhood of the young days was
transformed into a manufacturing association, the firm of
Morris & Company. That firm was the visible symbol
and the moving force of a silent revolution in the domestic
arts, and more than that, in the conditions under which
these arts are or ought to be practised. Its object,
briefly stated, was twofold : first and more particularly,
to reinstate decoration, down to all its details, as one of
the fine arts ; next and more widely, to reinstate art
itself as a function of common civic life and a vital element
in the organism of society. This is not the occasion to
speak of the actual products of the firm—its painted
windows, furniture, metal and glass work, tiles, cloth and

paper wall-hangings, jewellery and embroideries, woven and knotted carpets, printed cottons, silk damasks, and tapestries. Nor is it the occasion to speak of the particular industries which Morris at one time and another took up and mastered, in order to know their processes and recover their secrets—in particular those of weaving, dyeing, and printing, each of which in turn marked a definite period in his life. There was hardly one of the productive arts which he did not touch. There was none he touched into which he did not put fresh life, which he did not in some way or another bring back into vital connection with its finest traditions, which he did not reinstate as an art combining imagination with craftsmanship. There is no designer or decorative worker now alive who is not consciously or unconsciously influenced by Morris' work. His activity was incessant and ever-varying ; but throughout, it had the unity given by a central idea and a central purpose. That idea and purpose was the reconstitution of art as a function of human life, and the revitalisation of human life through art. Not only the house, the symbol and local centre of life, but the life lived in the house, was subject to this law. Morris' whole work, in its largest sense, was the application of design to life, so that life might become rational, harmonious, and beautiful. Art, as Morris understood it, was the joy of life ; and art by the people and for the people, a joy to the maker and the user, was the famous phrase in which he expressed his ideal.

This is not a mere digression ; for it has to be borne carefully in mind when we pass to the next main group of his poems, *Jason* and *The Earthly Paradise*. In that great mass of poetry—fifty or sixty thousand lines in all—he was applying, during three or four years of continuous production, this doctrine of art to language. It

was to decorate the life lived in the house with stories
beautifully told in musical words and through bright
images, just as the house was to be decorated with things
serviceable, shapely, beautifully designed and coloured.
He formed the scheme of a great body of romantic or
tragic stories, to be connected with one another by a
single large and most skilfully designed framework in
which they were set ; and to this whole scheme he gave
the name of *The Earthly Paradise*. *The Life and Death
of Jason* was originally meant to be one of these stories,
and to be included with the rest in the general framework.   But in this case the story was so large, and grew
so under his handling, that it became a separate romantic
epic by itself.   Other stories written for *The Earthly
Paradise* were left out, some because he was not satisfied
with them, others merely because the design was full
without them.   *The Earthly Paradise* as it stands consists of twenty-four stories in verse, two for each month
of the year, of which one is Greek and the other mediæval.
These are all supposed to be told towards the end of the
fourteenth century, that is to say, in Chaucer's time, in
an island among unexplored seas.   To that island the
survivors of a company of people who had left Europe
in flight from the Black Death have finally come, and
have found in it a Greek people who had lived there
ever since ancient times, cut off from the rest of the
world.   The company of wanderers had sailed in search
of some actual earthly paradise which was rumoured to
exist somewhere in the remote West ; the story of their
voyage itself, with all its adventures, makes a twenty-
fifth story in the whole poem, introducing the others.
The stories are here and there interspersed with lyrics,
and are connected with one another by beautiful transi-
tional pieces.   The whole structure of this vast body of

poetry is remarkable, indeed almost unexampled, for intricacy and ingenuity : an ingenuity so great that it seems all perfectly simple and straightforward ; and an intricacy handled with such mastery, with such a power over composition and design, that it never seems forced, and in fact is hardly noticed until attention is called to it. Thus it is part of the charm, and part of the value of *The Earthly Paradise*, that while it is a single complex and beautifully organised structure, in which the parts all bear relation to the whole, the parts themselves are detachable, and in the highest degree enjoyable. We can read the exquisite prologue and epilogue, or the verses on the months, or the songs which occur here and there in the stories, with delight by themselves and for their own sake ; and we can read any one of the stories as a complete poem. This is so with Chaucer's *Canterbury Tales* also ; the scheme of *The Earthly Paradise*, though much more elaborate, is in great measure suggested by them, and Morris always thought and spoke of Chaucer as his master, and as not only the best loved, but the greatest, or at all events equal to the greatest, of the English poets. When he placed the action of *The Earthly Paradise* in Chaucer's time, it was a way of indicating that in Chaucer English poetry had to Morris' mind reached perfection, and that poets must, so to speak, go back to Chaucer, and start afresh from that point, if that perfection were to be renewed and repeated.

The stories in *The Earthly Paradise* itself, leaving the *Jason* on one side, vary very much in scope and treatment. *Jason*, as I said, far outgrew its original plan ; it became a poem of more than ten thousand lines, giving completely, and with great richness and beauty, the whole of one of the five or six great stories of the world, the Quest of the Golden Fleece and the tale of Jason and

Medea. In scale it is an epic ; in treatment it is, not an epic, but a romance ; that is to say, it does not deal at high tension and concentration with a single great action, but is a narrative woven out of many actions, and combining the two great romantic motives of love and adventure, or, as we might call them in other words, the romance of situation and the romance of incident. One would naturally begin, in reading Morris, with some of the shorter, simpler, and more compact stories in *The Earthly Paradise* itself. Some of these, and not the least beautiful, can be read with delight even by children : for instance *The Writing on the Image*, or *The Lady of the Land*, or *The Fostering of Aslaug*, or above all *The Man born to be King*, a story of radiant beauty, most lucidly and exquisitely told. Others are more complex and make greater demands on the intelligence and imagina- tion : such are *The Ring given to Venus*, or *The Story of Cupid and Psyche*, or *The Land East of the Sun and West of the Moon*, with its tinge of mystery and its remarkable setting, one which had a great fascination for Morris, of a dream wakening into a dream so that the boundaries of dreamland and waking are lost. The longest of the stories in *The Earthly Paradise* is at the same time much the most remarkable, and in every way the greatest. This is *The Lovers of Gudrun* : and I must make some special mention of it, not only on its own account, but because it is the turning-point between Morris' earlier romantic and his later epic poetry. It stands in the very centre, and perhaps at the very head, of all his poetical work.

When Morris was writing the poems which are fitted together in the large framework of *The Earthly Paradise*, a new and powerful influence reached him, that of the Northern Sagas, the heroic literature of Iceland in

Iceland's great period, the eleventh and twelfth centuries. Those Sagas never had any effect on Europe at the time, and indeed were almost unknown beyond Iceland until last century. Now they are not only known, but recognised to be one of the great literatures of the world. Their writers combined two things, both of which are as rare as they are valuable : the narrative gift, and the heroic temper. They knew, by the instinct of genius, exactly how to tell a story most simply, most powerfully, and most vividly : they knew also, by a like instinct, not only how to tell stories, but what stories were worth telling. In that remote, thinly-peopled island, the Norse colonists or exiles who dwelt in it realised to the full the dramatic value and the essential greatness of human life. They realised this equally in the ancient traditions of the Northern Mythology which had come down among them, and in the actual life that passed before their eyes. Thus the best of their sagas, whether mythological like the *Volsunga-saga*, or historical like the *Njala* and *Grettis-saga*, are unequalled for truth and strength, for largeness of outlook and handling, and for the way in which they bring life before us as something wonderful, awful, and great.

It is one of those Icelandic stories, the *Laxdaela-saga*, which Morris retold in *The Lovers of Gudrun*. His whole heart went into it, and we may test our appreciation of Morris by the effect which it produces on us. Iceland became to him, after he came to know the Icelandic literature, a sort of holy country. He went there, and travelled over the scenes of its greatest stories, as soon as *The Earthly Paradise* was off his hands. That visit, and another he made two years later, made an indelible impression on him ; its traces may be seen in nearly all his later work. No long time after, he set to work on the great epic which I have mentioned as representing the third period in his poetry.

This epic of *Sigurd the Volsung and the Fall of the Niblungs* is his largest single work in poetry (if we do not count the whole of *The Earthly Paradise* as a single work, which of course in a sense it is), and the work which he himself thought not only his largest but his highest. As to this there may be, and have been, differences of opinion. They are based very largely on the fundamental and eternal differences of mental attitude towards life, and hence towards the interpretation of life given in books. The naturally romantic mind finds its affinity and ideal in romance, in the free movement of imagination over the pageant of things, with its two great leading motives of love and adventure ; the naturally epic mind in epic, with its concentration, its high tension, its pursuit of action rather than incident, of will and passion rather than charm and sentiment. Those who give the first place in Morris' work to his romances can point, with much justice, to the fact that it was in romance that he began, and to romance that he finally returned ; his epic period was in their view transitory, and due to what was really a deflecting influence. The same question may be raised with Shakespeare. He too began as a romantic dramatist, and ended again as one, in his loveliest plays, *The Tempest*, *The Winter's Tale*, *Cymbeline*. Yet most people would say that Shakespeare's greatest and most Shakespearean work was the high tragedy (and for that matter, the high comedy also) of his central period, where we have the quality corresponding in dramatic poetry to what is in narrative poetry the epic splendour, the epic concentration, the epic tension.

However we may think about this, Morris' *Sigurd* is among the noblest of English poems, as its subject is among the noblest which human experience and human imagination have shaped. As he himself says, in the preface to his translation of the *Volsunga-saga*, " This is the Great Story of the North, which should be to all our race what the Tale of Troy was to the Greeks." It is a story even greater than that of the *Iliad* and *Odyssey*, and " we cannot doubt," as he goes on to say, " that any reader of poetic insight will be intensely touched by finding, amidst all its wildness and remoteness, such a startling realism, such subtlety, such close sympathy with all the passions that may move himself to-day." Even more than that we may say ; for in Morris' version, into which he poured all of his own best, we shall find little less than a complete picture of the world, of life, of men and women, in all that makes men and women and life and the world most deeply great. Its spirit is concentrated in two passages above all. Even these are too long for me to quote, but I will quote out of them. One is the *Wisdom of Brynhild*, at the end of the second book of the poem :

—She told of the hidden matters whereby the world is moved,
And she told of the framing of all things, and the houses of the
    heaven,
And she told of the star-worlds' courses, and how the winds be
    driven,
And she spake of the love of women, and told of the flame that
    burns,
And the fall of mighty houses, and the friend that falters and
    turns,
And the lurking blinded vengeance, and the wrong that amendeth
    wrong,
And the hand that repenteth its stroke, and the grief that
    endureth for long,
And how man shall bear and forbear and be master of all that is,
And how man shall measure it all, the wrath and the grief and
    the bliss.

The other is the song of Gunnar at the end of the poem, when he is awaiting his death in the worm-pit of King Atli :

On the Thrones are the Powers that fashioned, and they name
    the night and the day,
And the tide of the moon's increasing, and the tide of his waning
    away,
And they name the years for the story ; and the lands they
    change and change,
The great and the mean and the little, that this unto that may
    be strange.

There were twain, and they went upon earth, and were speech-
    less, unmighty and wan,
They were hopeless, deathless, lifeless, and the Mighty named
    them Man.
Then they gave them speech and power, and they gave them
    colour and breath,
And deeds and the hope they gave them, and they gave them
    Life and Death :
Yea, hope, as the hope of the Framers : yea, might, as the
    Fashioners had,
Till they wrought, and rejoiced in their bodies, and saw their
    sons and were glad.
And they changed their lives and departed, and came back as
    the leaves of the trees
Come back and increase in the summer : and I, I, I am of these.
I have dwelt in the world aforetime, and I called it the Garden
    of God ;
I have stayed my heart with its sweetness, and fair on its fresh-
    ness I trod :
I have seen its tempest and wondered, I have cowered adown
    from its rain,
And desired the brightening sunshine, and seen it and been fain.
I have waked, time was, in its dawning ; its noon and its even
    I wore ;
I have slept unafraid of its darkness, and the days have been
    many and more.
I have dwelt with the deeds of the mighty ; I have woven the
    web of the sword :

I have borne up the guilt nor repented ; I have sorrowed nor
  spoken the word ;
And I fought and was glad in the morning, and I sing in the
  night and the end.

Years after he wrote this poem, Morris said, in a letter
to a friend, " It seems to me that no hour of the day
passes that the whole world does not show itself to me."
This wonderful vision of his he enables us in some degree
to share, if we read and understand his books.   It is a
vision like that of Sigurd and Brynhild from the mountain
top in this same poem :

For far away beneath them lie the kingdoms of the earth
And the garths of men-folk's dwellings, and the streams that
  water them,
And the rich and plenteous acres, and the silver ocean's hem,
And the woodland wastes and the mountains, and all that
  holdeth all,
The house and the ship and the island, the loom and the mine
  and the stall,
The beds of bane and healing, the crafts that slay and save,
The temple of God and the Doom-ring, the cradle and the
  grave.

If we go back from a passage like this to Morris' earlier
romantic poetry and the world of romance which it embodies, we shall see what a long road he had travelled
between them.   Take, for instance, the song of the
Hesperides in *Jason* :

Lo, such as is this garden green,
In days past all the world has been,
And what we know all people knew
Save this, that unto worse all grew.
  But since the golden age is gone,
This little place is left alone,
Unchanged, unchanging, watched of us
The daughters of wise Hesperus.
  Nor will we have a slave or king,
Nor yet will we learn anything

But that we know, that makes us glad,
While oft the very gods are sad
With knowing what the Fates shall do.
　Neither from us shall wisdom go
To fill the hungering hearts of men,
Lest to them threescore years and ten
Come but to seem a little day
Once given, and taken soon away.
Nay, rather, let them find their life
Bitter and sweet, fulfilled of strife,
And surely when all this is past
They shall not want their rest at last.
　Let earth and heaven go on their way
While still we watch from day to day,
In this green place left all alone,
A remnant of the days long gone.

That beautiful still dream-world has become, in the
later poem, a world that learns and suffers, that moves
and is alive. It is no less wonderful ; it is, though in
another way, no less beautiful ; but now it is no dream,
it is a reality ; it has become a world of vast movements,
tragic passions, elemental forces.

Beyond epic, poetry cannot go. I do not mean, of
course, to set one kind of poetry against another, still
less to say that any one kind of poetry—be it the lyric,
or the ballad, or the idyll, or what not—is, compared with
epic, an imperfect kind of poetry, poetry that is less
poetical. There are many different forms of art that may
be perfect, and in that sense there are many kinds of perfection. But what I mean is, that in the epic, poetry is
on its amplest scale and makes its most royal progress.
A little piece of half a dozen or a dozen lines by Blake
or Shelley, a single sonnet of Shakespeare's, a song by
Burns, may be as perfect in its kind, may be as essentially
and vitally poetry of the highest order, as the *Iliad* or the
Paradise Lost. But the epic towers above them by its

mere size and amplitude.   In this it has only one rival,
the poetical drama ; for that too may be on the heroic
scale.   Morris wrote little dramatic poetry ; his choice
did not lie that way.   In *The Defence of Guenevere* there
is a very beautiful dramatic fragment, *Sir Peter Harpdon's
End ;* and between *The Earthly Paradise* and *Sigurd,*
when he was experimenting in different forms, he wrote
the dramatic poem called *Love is Enough,* a work of
great beauty, but rather difficult reading for inexperi-
enced readers, and bearing in it the traces of being what
it was, an experiment rather than an accomplished
masterpiece.   That is about all.   Soon after his death,
Mr. Shaw said of him, quite truly as I think, " If he had
started a Kelmscott Theatre instead of the Kelmscott
Press, I am quite confident that in a few months, without
going half a mile afield for his company, he would have
produced work that would within ten years have affected
every theatre in Europe."   But this he did not do,
because he did not choose to do it.   You may notice
about Morris—and it is part of the secret of his greatness
—that throughout his life he nearly always knew exactly
what he liked, and did that.

But when I spoke just now about the vision of the
whole world that he always had before him, and that he
put into splendid poetry at the culminating points of
Sigurd, the word reminds me that poetry at its highest
reach tends to transcend the limits of both romance and
epic, both lyric and drama, and to become, in the full
sense of the word, a vision.   You will find this happening
in the work of many of the greatest poets.   It happens
in Virgil's *Aeneid* ; it happens in Milton's *Paradise Lost.*
In Shelley it is constantly happening.   Keats was deliberately turning his *Hyperion* into a vision just before
he was struck down by his fatal illness.   Dante is in

some respects perhaps the greatest of all the poets ; and his poem, though he himself called it a comedy (the name of Divine Comedy was given to it after his death), and though others have called it an epic, is not either in any ordinary sense of the words, and is, what it has also often been formally entitled, a vision—the vision of the invisible world of Hell, Purgatory, and Paradise.

Morris too wrote his vision of the invisible world ; but it was in prose, not in poetry ; and it was not the invisible world of Hell and Heaven, but of this world, nay more, of this England, in the vanished past and in the unseen future. " Of Heaven and Hell I have no power to sing," he wrote in the first line of the famous verses prefixed to *The Earthly Paradise*. That was because Heaven and Hell, as one might say, did not interest him : it was this earth that he cared for, " the earth," as he said, " that I love and worship." His vision is that exquisite little book, the very heart of Morris' work, *A Dream of John Ball*. That is Morris himself, in so far as a man can exist in, and so to speak put himself fully into, written words. I will not say more about it, except just this : that whatever of Morris you read, this you ought to read, and this you must read if you would understand Morris.

To this review of Morris' writings a few words may be added about the power that was behind the writings, about Morris himself.

And first I will quote two of Morris' own sayings, both very short and very simple, but both coming deep out of his own heart and both going deep into the heart of life. They are easy to remember, and are worth remembering. At the age of twenty-one, while he was still at Oxford, and when the beauty and the meaning and the call of life were opening before him, he wrote to his mother, " I will by no means give up things I have thought of for the bettering of the world in so far as lies in me." Once more, at the age of forty-two, in the full prime of his powers and of his work and fame, he wrote again to his dearest friend, " I entreat you to think that life is not empty nor made for nothing, and that the parts of it fit into one another in some way." These two sentences are the keynotes of his life and work. More than that: they give the basis, and the guiding idea, not only of Morris' work as an artist and poet, as a manufacturer and designer, but of what lay behind that, Morris' Socialism.

For to him Socialism meant the bettering of the world, and the making the parts of life fit into one another. Co-operation towards this end in a common spirit, in a common faith and hope, lay with him not merely at the heart of production, but at the heart of life. Without it, life was, in the proper sense of the word, hell. " He that waketh in hell," he makes John Ball say, " and feeleth his heart fail him, shall have memory of the merry days of earth and how that when his heart failed him there, he cried on his fellow, and how that his fellow heard him and came. This shall he think on in hell, and cry on his fellow to help him, and shall find that therein is no help because there is no fellowship, but every man for himself." And as life without fellowship is hell, so life with fellowship is nothing less than heaven. The great fellowship of a fully socialised commonwealth, whether it be a far-off dream felt after in the darkness, or a clear vision of what is just through the door, waiting to be entered into, is the dream or vision of a kingdom of God on earth.

This is Morris' Earthly Paradise. In the poem so named, he tells the story of a search for an Earthly

Paradise in some particular place : it was searched for
and not found, because it did not exist. For Dante, such
a place did exist ; he was quite sure and precise about
it : it was on the Mountain of Purgatory, in the southern
hemisphere, just opposite Jerusalem. We know now that
there is no such place : at that spot there is no Mountain
of Purgatory and no Earthly Paradise, but only the empty
Pacific Ocean under the Low Archipelago. For Morris,
the Heaven and Hell of Dante had also faded away.
Heaven and Hell were here. In the Paradise of the
theologians, as in their other dogmas, he had ceased to
believe. That was a Paradise which lay outside of this
world ; which remedied—if it did remedy—the wrong
and misery of this world by abolishing this world itself.
The finding and winning of an Earthly Paradise which
should *be* this world itself was the goal towards which,
more and more clearly as life went on, he set his eyes,
and towards which he set the eyes of those who will
understand and follow him. Fellowship upon this earth,
as this earth was meant to be, and might be, was all he
desired and all he could conceive of heaven. Turn now
again to the lines which stand at the beginning of *The
Earthly Paradise* and let us read them with fuller appreciation of their meaning :

> Of Heaven and Hell I have no power to sing,
> I cannot ease the burden of your fears,
> Or make quick-coming death a little thing,
> Or bring again the pleasure of past years,
> Nor for my words shall ye forget your tears,
> Or hope again for aught that I can say,
> The idle singer of an empty day.

Morris calls these verses an Apology. They are his last
cry out of the darkness before he reached the light. For
the whole message and meaning of his life and work

thereafter was just this : to ease the burden of our fears by showing that our fears are shadows ; to make death a less thing than life ; to bring the pleasure of past years back to a world that had lost it ; to make men hope again. This is what he holds up before us, as a hope and a faith : the arts re-created and knit together into one vital organic art filling life ; the people re-born and knit together into one commonwealth ; the coming of mankind into its inheritance ; life not empty nor made for nothing, and the parts of it fitting into one another. Meanwhile, he carried on his own work patiently from day to day, and exhorted others by word and example to carry on theirs ; " not living like fools and fine gentlemen, and not beaten by the muddle, but like good fellows trying by some dim candle-light to set our workshop ready against to-morrow's daylight." Do you see how these words repeat, with a difference, those of that exquisite early lyric which I have already cited ?

Patiently waiting there for the dawn,
Patient and colourless, though heaven's gold
Waits to float through them along with the sun.

It is the same voice that speaks ; but now the cloudy romance has become a clear dream and solemn vision.

The lesson which Morris impressed most deeply on those who knew him is not to be found in his poems, nor in his handicraft, nor even in his express teaching of Socialism. It was the lesson of a life lived simply, courageously, and straightforwardly : a life without false shame, without self-seeking, and guided by an almost childlike dutifulness. His final message to us rests upon two words—Courage and Hope. All his life he had been trying to do what, as time went on, he saw more and more clearly was, in the actual conditions of things, impossible. But that was only a reason the more for altering the actual conditions of things, not for losing hope or faltering in courage. In an unpublished and unfinished story, Morris says, while describing the boyhood of the principal figure in it, which is really himself, "He began to dream about it, as his way was about everything, to make it something different from what it was." To make things different from what they are, to bring out the pattern from their confusion, is the essential work alike of the poet, the craftsman, and the reformer. And thus it is that the "dreamer of dreams born out of my due time," as he described himself in a famous line, was also the most effective and practical of men, and has put his impress on the whole movement of the world. His due time was to-morrow's daylight, against which he bids us set our workshop ready, as he set his. In the words of another ringing sentence of his own, "It is for him that is lonely or in prison to dream of fellowship, but for him that is of a fellowship to do and not to dream. He who doeth well in fellowship and because of fellowship, shall not fail, though he seem to fail to-day, but in days hereafter shall he and his work yet be alive." Morris and his work are thus alive now.

SWINBURNE

A LECTURE DELIVERED BEFORE THE UNIVERSITY
OF OXFORD, 30 APRIL 1909

SWINBURNE

It was no part of my scheme of lectures from this Chair to give any account, or offer any matured criticism, of poets of our own time. That is a thing that can be better done when they have fallen into perspective, when the dust of contemporary praise or blame has settled from round them, and they have taken their place among the ranks of the immortals, those who, in the words of Simonides, οὐ τεθνᾶσι θανόντες, being dead are yet alive. But the death of Algernon Charles Swinburne has placed him in this rank ; and while it may be yet too early to fix his place among the English poets, or to say with confidence how much of his poetry will remain living and classic, his place somewhere among them is assured, and his influence on the whole poetical movement of his age is no less certain than profound. Last Easter Eve marks not only the death of a poet but the end of an age in poetry : that age of which he called himself, forty-five years ago, the youngest singer, and of which he lived to be the last. Of the six great Victorian poets it is legitimate to remember here, in piety as well as in pride, that three were sons of Oxford ; and I may be allowed to remember also that two of them were of my own College. Swinburne's name is not indeed, like Arnold's, connected inseparably with Oxford ; he went down without taking a degree, nor did he receive, in the years of his later fame, any public recognition from his mother-university. But his name still appears on the University Register of Honours as Taylorian Scholar : and of the ancient literature which we here make our especial study, no less than of the French and Italian in which he gained his own University distinction, he was an accomplished master, a distinguished scholar in the classical sense of that word. It is therefore in every way no less than right that he should receive here some valediction and commemoration.

I do not propose in discharging this duty to attempt anything in the nature of a biography of Swinburne. In any case the facts of his life are few and simple, for it was one which from first to last was devoted to letters, and never came before the public. He prided himself, quietly and not unjustly, on his descent by both parents from a distinguished ancestry ; and he inherited fully the aristocratic instinct which is reticent of its private affairs and shrinks from anything like display or self-advertisement. No man of letters of equal eminence has lived in our own times who has been less in the newspapers and less in what is called the world. He lived in London, but lived his own life ; and the deafness which came on him in middle life combined with his dislike of publicity to make him something of a recluse. Of his earlier years, and the circle of which he was then the youngest and one of the most brilliant members, there are fragmentary records in the published memorials of those among them who predeceased him, notably of Rossetti, Morris, and Burne-Jones. By the few survivors of that circle his memory is cherished for qualities which did not, and need not, come before the public ; for transparent simplicity, unbounded affectionateness, and steady loyalty : and mingling with all these, and with his excitable impetuousness, an old-fashioned and charming courtesy. Nor would any estimate of Swinburne be true which did not take into account his habitual attitude of adoration towards infancy and of reverence for old age.

But this is matter for his biographer, in so far as it is not too intimate even for published biography. At all events it is not of Swinburne's personality that I wish to speak here, but of his poetry, and incidentally of his criticism. For he was one of the great poets who have also been fine and penetrating critics, and his volumes of published criticism—his studies of Blake, of Chapman, of the other Elizabethans, and, above all, of Shakespeare—are not only the outcome of wide knowledge and deep study, but the direct and sincere expression of a very remarkable mind. They cannot be neglected or ignored by any student of ancient or modern poetry. He put new life into poetical criticism, gave it a new range and scope and brilliance, in something of the same way as he discovered or revealed new potentialities in poetry itself.

The lives of the six great Victorian poets extend conjointly over just a century, from the birth of Tennyson, the eldest of them, in 1809, to the death of Swinburne, the youngest, in this year. It is to the latter half of that century that the poetry of Swinburne belongs. His first published volume—he was then twenty-four—was in 1861, just after the middle point of those hundred years. In 1864, three years later, he broke into the full blaze of fame by the publication of *Atalanta in Calydon*. From that time forward his production was continuous and incessant. The long list of his published writings in prose and verse only ends with last year. But the period of his vogue and predominance, that during which he was a formative and creative influence of the first rank, was that of the later 'sixties and the 'seventies. It begins suddenly and decisively with the *Atalanta* ; it rises to its full height

with the *Poems and Ballads* of 1866.   It remained steady
for ten or a dozen years more ; then it began to decline.
The two poetical volumes of 1880, *Songs of the Springtides*
and *Studies in Song*, marked the beginnings of a waning
popularity, or at least of a less assured hold upon the
poet's audience, which was hardly regained by *Tristram of
Lyonesse* two years later, and which in fact, when once lost,
is hardly recoverable.   The influence of his older work
continued, but was not augmented ; and, like all influences,
it gradually became absorbed, while at the same time
other voices arose with different messages.   From Swinburne's effective work in the history and progress of our
poetry we are thus already separated by some thirty years ;
and to the younger generation, if not to those who were
his readers and lovers then, it may perhaps be approaching
the point at which it takes something like a final place,
and can be submitted to what is provisionally at least a
definitive judgment.   For the older among us—those to
whom he was, or seemed to be, a contemporary—it is a
different matter.   When we look back, the old enchantment returns.   We can see those early poems now with
clearer eyes it may be, certainly with a more matured
judgment ; but when we return to them, we return to our
own youth ; we can only criticise them as the man beyond
middle life can criticise the boy who was so different from
him and yet who was himself.

Let me then take you back to the 'sixties, to the time
when Swinburne struck into English poetry with such
immediate and such decisive effect.   It was a time which
in poetry as in other fields of human energy was the turn
of the tide between two epochs, one might almost say
between two worlds.   The imposing external unity given
by the long reign of the late Queen to the period which
covers the last sixty years of the nineteenth century is apt

to conceal from us the fact that it really consists of two periods ; and that these, although the one merged gradually into the other, are nevertheless in sharp contrast as regards essentials. In politics, in the large movement of actual life, the earlier period was one of liberation and expansion ; the period which succeeded it was one of reaction and concentration. The war of 1870 between France and Prussia may be taken as the dividing line ; it separates, by events which were a spectacle for the whole world, an age of ideas, enthusiasms, and hopes from one of materialism and disillusion. I must not encroach on the province of my colleagues whose duty it is to study and interpret history : but just so much must be said, for all art is a function of life, and Swinburne's early achievement, as well as his later development, bears essential relation to the age in which he was born and the age into which he lived. He was the last flower in poetry of the earlier or mid-Victorian age ; he passes away now as its last or almost its last survivor ; and to this, unconscious witness is borne by the fact that even in recent years he continued to be instinctively thought of as one of the younger poets : not as one older, by nearly a generation, than others who write to-day, but rather as the younger colleague of Tennyson and Browning, of Arnold and Rossetti and Morris ; like the youngest brother in a fairy tale, whose youth is part of his definition, and who remains, so far as his place in the story is concerned, always a boy.

In the early 'sixties English poetry had come, for the time, to something of a standstill. New movements were under the surface, preparing to appear ; but meanwhile the heavy atmosphere of mid-Victorianism had settled down. Tennyson had, with the first four *Idylls of the King*, come into a popularity shared with Mrs. Browning

and Miss Ingelow, and with other writers, like Alexander
Smith, now almost forgotten. Browning, then at the
height of his powers, had but a small audience : the time
was indeed over when *Bells and Pomegranates* were brought
out in the form of paper-covered sixpenny pamphlets
because no more substantial volume could have sold
enough copies to cover the cost of production, but he
was still in the middle of those twenty years of neglect
which only began to lift with the publication, in 1868, of
The Ring and the Book. Rossetti was the centre of a small
group of men of genius whose work, owing much upon
many sides to his influence, was to effect a revolution in
the arts ; but his long-brooded-over and jealously-hoarded
volume did not appear till 1870, and until then he was,
beyond his own immediate circle, unknown. Arnold
was turning from poetry to criticism. Morris's first
volume had been published only to be left unnoticed, and
not even receive the compliment of abuse. The minor
poets, in whom (and that is perhaps their chief value, at
least after their own day) the general current of public
taste and poetical tendency can with some accuracy be
traced, mainly cultivated a sort of vapid and bloodless
Tennysonianism. The poetical atmosphere was exhausted and heavy, like that of a sultry afternoon darken-
ing to thunder. Out of that stagnation broke, all in
a moment, the blaze and crash of *Atalanta in Calydon.*
It was something quite new, quite unexampled. It
revealed a new language in English, a new world, as it
seemed, in poetry. The older Olympians shook their
heads and growled. Tennyson paid the new poetry one
or two guarded and rather acid compliments. Browning
spoke frankly of it as " a fuzz of words." Arnold was a
little petulant about it, and a little inclined to resent the
admiration given to *Atalanta* and refused to his own

Merope. But its brilliance disarmed and almost silenced criticism. Even the great quarterlies came lumbering up with tributes of amazed admiration seldom given by them to poetry, and seldomer still to a new poet.

Two years later were published the *Poems and Ballads*, and by this time public opinion, already made a little uneasy by *Chastelard*, was fully aroused and violently divided. The reception, even more than the appearance, of *Poems and Ballads*, marks a turning-point in literary history. From that point onwards Swinburne, violently assailed on the one hand as immoral, irreligious, and un-English, became on the other hand the master of a revolutionary school, the standard-bearer of a new Romanticism. On both sides, his fame and influence were secured. The *Poems and Ballads* were dedicated to Burne-Jones, in verses of exquisite melody and no less exquisite praise. The dedication connected the two names inseparably. With little in common beyond friendship, love of beauty, and enthusiasm for freedom, they became classed together by an indiscriminating public, together with Rossetti, after he became known through the *Poems* of 1870, as the hierophants of a strange art, exotic, mystic, fascinating, which evoked an almost adoring admiration from not a few, but by which the great bulk of opinion was perplexed and alarmed. This impression, as regards Swinburne, was intensified and fixed by the *Songs before Sunrise* of 1871. Against that volume no charge of indecency could be brought by the most ready malevolence. Its ethical loftiness was almost austere. But on other grounds it shocked traditional conservatism even more. Its profession of republicanism might have been passed over had it not been combined with attacks—for as such they were taken—on the most cherished English beliefs and institutions — with the exposition of Pantheism in *Hertha* and the envisagement of Christianity as a cruel superstition in *Before a Crucifix* and the *Hymn of Man*.   Much of the obloquy then poured on Swinburne seems now, a generation afterwards (like the obloquy which unhinged the mind of Rossetti, and through which Burne-Jones worked on steadily to win a late and grudging appreciation), to be almost grotesquely irrelevant.   But it was serious enough then ; it was the recoil against the prodigious impact of a new art, in hands of immense genius, upon a world in which the artistic sense had gone to sleep and could only be awakened by a shock that set all its nerves tingling.

Those seven years, 1864 to 1871, were the culminating period of Swinburne's production, as they were also the period of his most immediate and profound effect upon the art of poetry.   In the decade which followed he continued, but did not materially reinforce, the impression he had already made.   He was not one of those minds which mature slowly and master their art by assiduous practice. His poetical faculty passed through no long process of gestation : it sprang from his brain suddenly, radiant and full-armed.   In the case of no poet perhaps is there less difference, either in intellect or in craftsmanship, between the poetry of his youth and that of his later years.   The term of precocious applies to him in the full weight of its meaning : in that sudden swift development there is no delaying spring, no slow process of the seasons : " the young year flushes from leaf to flower and flower to fruit, and fruit and leaf are as gold and fire."   In the 'seventies *Bothwell* continues, and hardly varies, the subject and method of *Chastelard* ; *Erechtheus* varies, and hardly advances upon, the spirit and treatment of *Atalanta* ; the second series of *Poems and Ballads* resumes, with few new notes and with a certain loss of the first freshness, of the unrecapturable first surprise, the redundant accomplished melodiousness of its predecessor. He was turning in these years, as in a very different way Arnold had done likewise, from creation to criticism. Arnold, who was born with the schoolmaster in his blood and was himself employed in the service of the State, turned to actual life, its education, its politics, its religious dogma ; and even his poetry became, what in one of his brilliant half-truths he defined poetry itself to be, a criticism of life. Swinburne, a born man of letters who had (in the ordinary sense) little interest in public affairs or social movements, turned to literature ; and criticism of literature, appreciation of the poets, actually became the substance or motive of much of his poetry. Letters were to him three-fourths of life ; the poets were, in a closer sense than the rest of mankind, his own flesh and blood. His early reverence for Landor, his lifelong worship of Victor Hugo are but two of the most striking instances out of many. Of our own Elizabethan poetry his knowledge was enormous and his appreciation searching. The *Study of Shakespeare*, published in 1880, is one of those works of illuminating and creative criticism which take rank as classics, and this in spite of a prose style which would damn any work of less genius. Of him, as of few other critics, it may be said that, while his way of expressing himself is irritating and indefensible, his knowledge is complete and his judgment nearly faultless. In almost any single instance, if we disengage the actual judgment from the torrent of language in which it is launched forth, we shall find it right. The best of critics would do well to think twice and thrice before differing from Swinburne's decision as to authorship, or quality, or specific excellence of any work, any passage, nay, even any single phrase in poetry. I speak of the bare effective

P

judgment, of condemnation or comparison or approval. For in the expression of his opinions he was congenitally incapable of measured or tempered statement. His mind moved in superlatives ; he becomes ineffective through mere over-emphasis ; but if we have patience to plunge through the entanglement of epithets and antitheses that choke the sentences we shall find beneath the rhetoric an artistic insight of swift precision and luminous truth.

By this time Swinburne had not only established his reputation as a poet ; he had formed a school. In a good deal of his later work we may be inclined to feel that he himself has become one of his own school, that the poetical style which he had created, and which was so new and so captivating, has become a mannerism. But to the last it was a style of which he alone possessed the full secret. While he had enlarged the capacities, verbal, metrical, and rhythmical, of the English language as a poetical instrument for the hands of others, his touch and handling remained his own. Swinburnianism as a poet-ical fashion is already obsolete, and the poet survived his school. It is now nearly thirty years ago since a clever critic, the late Mr. H. D. Traill, wrote a series of parodies on contemporary poets, which might still be read with amusement and interest, but that they never, I think, were reprinted from the fugitive publication where they first appeared. Some of the verses put in Swinburne's mouth give, with a not unkindly malice, a criticism of real value. The amazed world is represented as coming to the poet and saying, " Master, how is it done ? " He answers that he cannot explain :

Let this thing serve you to know :
When the river of rhymes should flow
    I turn on the tap, and they come.

How it is done is by an incommunicable instinct or

aptitude. But how it is not done can be easily explained ;
he goes on to say of his imitators :

> They strut like jays in my lendings,
>   They chatter and screech : I sing.
> They mimic my phrases and endings,
>   And rum Old Testament ring :
> But the lyrical cry isn't in it,
> And the high gods spot in a minute
>   That it isn't the genuine thing.

The genuine thing his own writing always was ; it was
always sincere and even in a way curiously simple, with
the simplicity of an extraordinarily eloquent child who
makes no reservations or compromises, who has no acquired tact, whose mind is quite transparent. He has less
atmosphere than any other poet who approaches him in
eminence, unless it be the great French master who was
the god of his idolatry ; for Victor Hugo also, in the
midst of all his grandiose rhetoric and torrential verbiage,
has this same childlike simplicity. Handwriting, if not
an index to character, is often very characteristic ; and
Swinburne's handwriting throughout his life was like
that of a schoolboy.

Like a child's, his intelligence was swift and clear. But
language intoxicated him ; swept on and borne away
by sheer delight of verbal and metrical artifice, he lets
decoration overflood construction, and the thought, what
Rossetti in a much-quoted phrase called the fundamental
brain-work of poetry, can hardly sustain the masses of its
gorgeous drapery. And his effect on the reader, through
the sheer splendour of the workmanship, is something of
a similar intoxication.

> Thou shalt touch and make redder his roses
>   With juice not of fruit nor of bud ;
> When the sense in the spirit reposes
>   Thou shalt quicken the soul through the blood :

> In the daytime thy voice shall go through him,
>   In his dreams he shall feel thee and ache ;
> Thou shalt kindle by night and subdue him
>   Asleep and awake.

These lines, as you will all recognise, are from *Dolores*, that triumphant masterpiece of rhythm and diction which took the world by storm in 1866. They convey, with singular aptness, the actual effect which the *Poems and Ballads* had in thrilling, stimulating, and quickening the poetic sense of their generation. Much of that effect was in its nature temporary. I do not know to what extent those poems—*Laus Veneris*, *Anactoria*, the *Hymn to Proserpine*, *Faustine*, *Dolores*, *Ilicet*, to name the half-dozen pieces in the volume through which the new poetry acted with the most powerful and immediate effect upon its audience—still preserve their original potency for an age for which they have lost their first shock of novelty, to which they do not come now as the lifting of a veil and the discovery of a world of art previously unknown. I do not know how far they seem now, as some among the contents of the volume certainly do, faded and unreal. Sense swooning into nonsense, the cynical description which has been given of them, is one which can be, and at one time or another has been, given of many of the highest flights of poetry. But those poems, with the lapse of years, have taken on them a strange dream-like quality, something elusive and phantasmal.

> Love is not glad nor sorry, as I deem :
> Labouring he dreams, and labours in the dream,
>   Till, when the spool is finished, lo, I see
> His web, reeled off, curls and goes out like steam.

> Night falls like fire ; the heavy lights run low,
> And as they drop, my blood and body so
>   Shake as the flame shakes, full of days and hours
> That sleep not neither weep they as they go.

There is no change of cheer for many days,
But change of chimes high up in the air, that sways
   Rung by the running fingers of the wind,
And singing sorrows heard on hidden ways.

There sit the knights that were so great of hand,
The ladies that were queens of fair green land,
   Grown grey and black now, brought unto the dust,
Soiled, without raiment, clad about with sand.

To the most hauntingly melodious passages in a piece like *Dolores* it is impossible to attach any definite meaning ; they affect the intelligence through a sort of charm of the senses, by suggestions as vague as those of music, and as potent.

Who now shall content thee as they did,
   Thy lovers, when temples were built,
And the hair of the sacrifice braided,
   And the blood of the sacrifice spilt
In Lampsacus fervent with faces,
   In Aphaca red from thy reign,
Who embraced thee with awful embraces,
   Our Lady of Pain ?

Out of Dindymus heavily laden
   Her lions draw, bound and unfed,
A mother, a mortal, a maiden,
   A queen over death and the dead.
She is cold, and her habit is lowly,
   Her temple of branches and sods ;
Most fruitful and virginal, holy,
   A mother of gods.

She hath wasted with fire thine high places,
   She hath hidden and marred and made sad
The fair limbs of the Loves, the fair faces
   Of gods that were goodly and glad.
She slays, and her hands are not bloody,
   She moves like a moon in the wane,
White-robed, and thy raiment is ruddy,
   Our Lady of Pain.

Music, drifting and impalpable : but what music it is !

I have had occasion already more than once in this Chair to lay stress on the fact that Hellas and Italy are the only two European countries, beyond its own, from which English poetry, in all its varying progress, has drawn essential life and authentic inspiration. In *Atalanta in Calydon* the Hellenic influence, the Hellenic inspiration, is ubiquitous and patent. The Italian inspiration came to Swinburne later, and in a very different and very remarkable way.

Only persons past middle life can now remember, can know of their own knowledge at first hand, the place that Italy and the Italian movement held, for some twenty years in the middle of last century, in the imagination and heart of Europe, and more particularly of England. The Italian revolution saturated both politics and literature. " One would think," said Emile Ollivier in 1860, " there was no other question in the world than Italy." The Roman Republic of 1849, the story of which Mr. George Trevelyan has recently retold with a vividness like that of an actual eyewitness, had created an ideal which dominated a whole generation. Garibaldi, when he came to England in 1864, had a more than royal reception. Mrs. Browning, in the time of her immense popularity, had made the Italian cause and the Italian ideal familiar to all her countrymen. That cause and ideal had inspired much of the poetry by which Browning himself won his way slowly to public appreciation. The Sicilian and Neapolitan campaigns of 1860, which even now read like a fairy-tale, dazzled the imagination of their own time ; to many thousands of Englishmen the names of Aspromonte and Mentana brought later a feeling of something like wounded national honour, something like the

anguish of a personal shame. We may read the enthusiasms of that epoch, outside of poetry, in works so
different as Mr. Meredith's *Vittoria* and Disraeli's *Lothair*.
For the enthusiasts of the progressive and revolutionary
movement throughout Europe the names of Italy and of
freedom were so closely linked that they were as one.

> —Men wept, saying *Freedom*, knowing of thee,
>   Child, that thou wast not free.

The Austrian butchers and the renegade Pope were not
merely the symbols, but the actual incarnation of moral
and spiritual death.

> As of one buried deep among the dead,
>   " Yea, she hath been," they said :
> " Far seasons and forgotten years enfold
>   Her dead corpse old and cold."
> With wings that widened and with beak that smote,
>   So shrieked through either throat
> From the hot horror of its northern nest
>   That double-headed pest ;
> So, triple-crowned with fear and fraud and shame,
>   He, of whom treason came.

On Swinburne the Italian enthusiasm had taken hold
from his youth ; and it was kindled to flame by admiration for the Italian exiles—many of them men of noble
character and impressive personality—who had sought
shelter in this country ; and beyond all the rest for
Mazzini, the man whom half Europe execrated as an
assassin and the other half revered as a prophet and saint.
The *Songs before Sunrise* are dedicated, in verses of splendid homage, to Mazzini : they are penetrated throughout
by the Italian enthusiasm ; and in them the best qualities
of Swinburne's poetry reach a height even beyond that of
his earlier work, and one which they never afterwards
surpassed, if indeed they ever afterwards equalled. With

all his unbounded admiration of the Greek poets and his unparalleled aptitude for recreating and revivifying the Hellenic forms, he was more a Latin than a Greek : he read Greek, as one might put it, with the eyes of the Italian Renaissance. I may illustrate what I mean by quoting from the most Greek, and one of the most beautiful, of the lyrics in *Atalanta*.

> For against all men from of old
> Thou hast set thine hand as a curse,
> And cast out gods from their places.
> These things are spoken of thee.
> Strong kings and goodly with gold
> Thou hast found out arrows to pierce,
> And made their kingdoms and races
> As dust and surf of the sea.
> All these, overburdened with woes
> And with length of their days waxen weak,
> Thou slewest ; and sentest moreover
> Upon Tyro an evil thing,
> Rent hair and a fetter and blows
> Making bloody the flower of the cheek,
> Though she lay by a god as a lover,
> Though fair, and the seed of a king.
> For of old, being full of thy fire,
> She endured not longer to wear
> On her bosom a saffron vest,
> On her shoulder an ashwood quiver,
> Being mixed and made one through desire
> With Enipeus, and all her hair
> Made moist with his mouth, and her breast
> Filled full of the foam of the river.

The phrasing and diction here are conspicuously Greek ; but the colour is that of Greek reinterpreted and re-embodied by the Western mind, seen across the Middle Ages and the whole of Latin and Gothic Art, and through a newly-charged medium. Its descent is from Athens, but its affinity is with the humanists. In the sister art it bears kinship to the work, not of the Greek masters, but of Giorgione or Titian. Or one may realise the difference if one compares Swinburne as a reinterpreter of Hellenic art with Leopardi, the one Italian poet who had a genius naturally and instinctively Greek.

In one of the *Songs before Sunrise* Swinburne pays a noble tribute to Leopardi, contrasting at the same time the sadness and weariness of the older poet with the new flush of youth, of hope, of exultation which had since come into the *Risorgimento*. Before the impassioned vision of Mazzini, and of those whom he inspired by his ardour, there shone nothing less than a new heaven and a new earth. Sunrise seemed actually at hand. The world, by one immense movement of common consciousness, was about to lift itself out of the darkness of ages. Tyranny and priestcraft were to disappear with selfishness and ignorance. Fear and her child Cruelty were to be struck down by the same blow ; in the name of God and the People the dreams of prophets, poets, and patriots were to flower into fulfilment. A little while, and Italy would rise from the sleep that was already broken and a world-wide Republic gather round the summoning standard of Rome. Of that exultant hope Swinburne was the lyric voice.

> Her hope in her heart was broken,
>   Fire was upon her, and clomb,
> Hiding her, high as her head,
> And the world went past her and said
> (We heard it say) she was dead :
> And now, behold, she hath spoken,
>   She that was dead, saying " Rome."
>
> O mother of all men's nations,
>   Thou knowest if the deaf world heard !
> Heard not now to her lowest
> Depths, where the strong blood slowest

Beats at her bosom, thou knowest,
In her toils, in her dire tribulations,
    Rejoiced not, hearing the word.

    •   •   •   •   •

Serve not for any man's wages,
    Pleasure nor glory nor gold ;
Not by her side are they won
Who saith unto each of you : " Son,
Silver and gold have I none ;
I give but the love of all ages,
    And the life of my people of old."

Turn ye, whose anguish oppressing you
    Crushes, asleep and awake,
For the wrong which is wrought as of yore,
That Italia may give of her store,
Having these things to give and no more,
Only her hands on you, blessing you,
    Only a pang for her sake :

Only her bosom to die on,
    Only her heart for a home,
And a name with her children to be
From Calabrian to Adrian sea
Famous in cities made free,
That ring to the roar of the lion
    Proclaiming republican Rome.

It was a false dawn ; and the splendours of it were just
caught by Swinburne before they faded into the light of
common day. These raptures and exultations must
seem, one fancies, " but an ashen-grey delight " to the
generation that has grown up since 1870. Even before
this volume of lyrics was published, the wonderful movement that inspired it had ceased to exist. The unification
of Italy was accomplished, almost without notice, while
the world's eyes were elsewhere, but it was not what
Mazzini had meant : and the cannonade of the Porta
Pia, as Carlyle says of the grapeshot of the 13 Vendé-

miaire just three-quarters of a century earlier, blew the
Revolution into the air. In the noble and little understood *Prelude* to the *Songs before Sunrise* the poet bids
farewell gravely and sadly, but courageously, to those
beautiful enthusiasms and vanished dreams, as well as to
the earlier raptures of his poetical boyhood.

> For what has he whose will sees clear
> To do with doubt and faith and fear ?
> His soul is even with the sun
> Whose spirit and whose eye are one.
> For Pleasure slumberless and pale,
> And Passion with rejected veil
> Pass, and the tempest-footed throng :
> So keen is change, and time so strong
> To weave the robes of life and rend
> And weave again till life have end.
> But weak is change, but strengthless time
> To take the light from heaven, or climb
> The hills of heaven with wasting feet.
> Songs they can stop that earth found meet,
> Actions and agonies control,
> And life and death, but not the soul :
> Because man's soul is man's God still
> What wind soever waft his will.
> Across the waves of day and night
> To port or shipwreck, left or right,
> Save his own soul's light overhead
> None leads him and none ever led.

It may be indeed that the judgment which Swinburne
here implicitly passes on his own earlier poetry will be
confirmed, and that in his later work, in his " Songs after
Sunrise," the fullest accomplishment of his genius will be
found. I have noticed that in the appreciations—many
of them generous and even enthusiastic, although a tendency is common in them to praise half-heartedly and to
slip unconsciously into a tone of apology—which have
been appearing since his death, it is the later poetry from

which passages are mainly cited ; and one cannot suppose that this is because the writers were unfamiliar with the earlier.   FitzGerald, you will remember, never could be got to admit that Tennyson had written anything really first-rate after 1842 : he missed, he said, the old champagne flavour ; and he did not inquire very closely whether the difference were in the wine or in the palate. But certainly Swinburne's later poetry, while its manner is apt to become mannerism and its substance appears often to be a mere variation—sometimes almost a repetition—of previous work, contains in it work of the highest kind ; and while years never taught him economy of rhythm or temperance in language or any marked increase of structural quality, they never took away from him the enthusiasm, the ardour, the high idealism of youth.   He sowed with the whole sack, in the Greek phrase ; but what he scattered so lavishly was his best ; and his best was incomparable.

The turning-point between the earlier and the later half of his poetical production may be taken as being the *Tristram of Lyonesse* volume of 1882.   Soon after its appearance, William Morris, writing to a friend, let fall a phrase which deserves close attention.   " Swinburne's work," he says, " always seemed to me to be grounded on literature, not on nature."   Here Morris laid his finger on what is, however we may regard it, an essential characteristic of Swinburne's poetry.   It does not imply either insincerity or artificiality : what it implies is a particular attitude towards life.   " Swinburne's sympathy with literature," Morris goes on to say in the letter from which I have just quoted, " is most genuine and complete ; and it is a pleasure to hear him talk about it, which he does in the best vein possible ; he is most steadily enthusiastic about it."   These words are both generous and discrimi-

nating : and they add weight to what Morris goes on to
say, which is this : " Time was when the poetry resulting
merely from this intense study and love of literature
might have been, if not the best, yet at any rate very
worthy and enduring : but in these days, when the issue
is so momentous and the surroundings of life so stern
that nothing can take serious hold of people, or should
do so, but that which is rooted deepest in reality and is
quite at first hand, there is no room for anything which is
not forced out of a man because of its innate strength and
vision."

In these words Morris, in his usual simple and direct
way, which never let him become entangled in techni-
calities, goes straight to the heart of the whole matter.
So far as poetry is founded on literature, not on nature, so
far as it is an interpretation not of life but of some interpretation of life already given, to that extent it is, with
whatever beauty of form or excellence of workmanship,
only art of the second order.   To this second order much
of Swinburne's poetry clearly belongs ; what makes it
still unique in its quality, what gives it still a substantive
and primary value, is that for him the world of literature
was more real, more alive, than the actual world.   In
dealing with books he was at the full stretch of interest,
of enthusiasm, of insight.   It is in dealing with actual life
that he produces, often though not always, a curious effect
of moving among abstractions, of seeing men and things
as books walking.   His vision of nature is conveyed
through a limited number of conventionalised symbols ;
the convention is beautiful and masterly, but we always
feel it to be a convention.   The rare instances where he
transcribes from nature (as in the little poem called *The
Sundew* in *Poems and Ballads,* or in touches elsewhere, as
in the description of the sunset gleaming through fine rain

at the end of the first section of *Tristram of Lyonesse*) produce a sort of shock of surprise.   When he attempts to
draw a scene more elaborately, as in *A Channel Passage*,
he becomes confused and involved and rhetorical.   He
had not in any large degree either the descriptive or the
narrative gift.   Nor had he the dramatic gift, in spite of
his great dramatic insight.   Half of his poetry is couched
in the dramatic form, from *Atalanta* and *Chastelard* onwards to *Rosamund, Queen of the Lombards* and *The Duke
of Gandia*, but it is all essentially lyrical ; it nowhere has
the distinctive dramatic creativeness ; it does not embody
human beings and show them developing character
through the interplay of will and passion.   In *Locrine* one
whole scene consists of a continuous series of sonnets.
From one point of view that is an almost childish trick, a
fanciful *tour de force* : from another it is an index and
symbol of the way in which the irrepressible lyrical genius
broke through and overbore everything else.   He was a
lyrist who tried to extend the lyrical method over the
whole field of poetry.   But that cannot be done ; and that
is why so much of his quasi-lyrical poetry, dramatic,
narrative, and critical, is neither one thing nor the other,
remains ineffective, and is not, so far as one can judge,
destined to immortality.

Of his purely lyrical work, where he was following and
not forcing the native bent of his own specific genius,
no praise could well be too high.   Its range is great, its
melody wonderful, its dexterity incomparable.   Perhaps
the third series of *Poems and Ballads*, published in 1889,
shows the variety and completeness of his lyrical gift most
strikingly.   In that small volume are included characteristic specimens of Swinburne at his best.   It includes
the splendid ode, written with all his earlier brilliance, and
with an unusual dignity and gravity, in celebration of the

Victorian Jubilee of 1887 : the tercentenary ode on the defeat of the Armada, where subject and treatment give full scope and justification for his opulence of language and magnificence of long rhythms : some of his most beautiful lyrics on children, and on dead friends : and those Northumbrian ballads, *The Tyneside Widow* and *A Jacobite's Exile*, which show Swinburne at his very highest excellence, for in them there is not only the familiar beauty of exquisite melody and faultless diction, but what we are apt to miss elsewhere, the warmth of a direct contact with earth.

The progress of poetry since the Victorian age has been tentative and dubious, at least to eyes still full of the splendour of an earlier day ; and certainly no great new school of poetry has arisen since, no single great poet broken upon the world with an immediate and profound impression, as Swinburne himself broke upon it in the 'sixties. In that ode which I have just mentioned *The Commonweal*, an age which is one of the most remarkable in human history is commemorated not less justly than nobly :

Hope, wild of eye and wild of wing,
    Rose with the sundawn of a reign
    Whose grace should make the rough ways plain,
And fill the worn old world with spring
    And heal its heart of pain.

Love, armed with knowledge, winged and wise,
    Should hush the wind of war, and see,
    They said, the sun of days to be
Bring round beneath serener skies
    A stormless jubilee.

Strange clouds have risen between, and wild
    Red stars of storm that lit the abyss
    Wherein fierce fraud and violence kiss
And mock such promise as beguiled
    The fiftieth year from this.

War upon war, change after change,
  Hath shaken thrones and towers to dust,
  And hopes austere and faiths august
Have watched in patience stern and strange
  Men's works unjust and just.

The morning comes not, yet the night
  Wanes, and men's eyes win strength to see
  Where twilight is, where light shall be,
When conquered wrong and conquering right
  Acclaim a world set free.

She, first to love the light, and daughter
  Incarnate of the northern dawn,
  She, round whose feet the wild waves fawn
When all their wrath of warring water
  Sounds like a babe's breath drawn,

How should not she best know, love best,
  And best of all souls understand
  The very soul of freedom, scanned
Far off, sought out in darkling quest
  By men at heart unmanned ?

The sea, divine as heaven and deathless,
  Is hers, and none but only she
  Hath learnt the sea's word, none but we
Her children hear in heart the breathless
  Bright watchword of the sea.

She gazes till the strenuous soul
  Within the rapture of her eyes
  Creates, or bids awake, arise,
The light she looks for, pure and whole
  And worshipped of the wise.

Such sons are hers, such radiant hands
  Have borne abroad her lamp of old,
  Such mouths of honey-dropping gold
Have sent across all seas and lands
  Her fame as music rolled.

To a poet who has spoken thus in praise of England,
the praise of England is surely due. This is the praise
which here we have the right to give him.

I said that I would not attempt any more intimate appreciation or say anything personal or biographical. But one little picture of him in his youth I should like to quote ; for it is drawn, long afterwards, by one who has clear large eyes to see and a delicate hand to portray. In her reminiscences of 1860, Lady Burne-Jones writes as follows :

Swinburne was the next remarkable personality I remember in these days [the early days of her own marriage]. He had rooms very near us, and we saw a great deal of him ; sometimes twice or three times in a day he would come in, bringing his poems hot from his heart and certain of welcome and a hearing at any hour. His appearance was very unusual and in some ways beautiful, for his hair was glorious in abundance and colour and his eyes indescribably fine. When repeating poetry he had a perfectly natural way of lifting them in a rapt, unconscious gaze, and their clear green colour softened by thick brown eyelashes was unforgettable : " looks commercing with the skies " expresses it without exaggeration. He was restless beyond words, scarcely standing still at all and almost dancing as he walked, while even in sitting he moved continually, seeming to keep time, by a swift movement of the hands at the wrists, and sometimes of the feet also, with some inner rhythm of excitement. He was courteous and affectionate and unsuspicious, and faithful beyond most people to those he really loved. The biting wit which filled his talk so as at times to leave his hearers dumb with amazement always spared one thing, and that was an absent friend.

It is a pleasant picture to end with, and we may end with it, rather than with any eulogy that would be inadequate. When the news came to Athens of the death of Euripides, Sophocles, we are told, put on mourning and made his chorus and actors appear in the Odeum ungarlanded. No one survives now to do a like honour to the last of the great Victorian poets.

TENNYSON
1923

TENNYSON

THERE is special reason to study Tennyson now ; and special circumstances which make the study of him more illuminating, and the resulting appreciation both of his poetical quality and of his effective poetical achievement more accurate, than it could have been at an earlier time. He is far enough away to have taken shape and perspective ; but not as yet so far that his world, his language, or his art has become unfamiliar. The mass and outline of him can be grasped as a whole, while as regards his aims and methods we are neither obliged nor tempted, as with poets of more distant ages, to fall back on conjectural reconstruction.

No final judgment can, of course, be passed on any artist ; the pendulum continues to swing ; or, as one might put it, the reality is neither the work of art nor the mind which approaches it, but the relation between the two ; and that relation is in perpetual flux. As regards Tennyson, the pendulum swung repeatedly in his own lifetime, and more violently still afterwards. He met with alternate idolatry and depreciation. Towards the close of the nineteenth century a strong reaction set in against Victorianism in all its aspects. He was the representative Victorian poet. Not only was he, alike in his virtues and in his defects, intensely English ; he was, beyond all others, the mouthpiece and interpreter

of his own contemporaries.   The position which this
gave him at the time can never recur ; a new age must
have new poetry of its own to live upon, must make its
own interpretation of life.   But it can only at its peril
neglect the great poets of the past.   Twenty or thirty
years ago it became the fashion not merely (which was
reasonable) to seek in poetry for other things than
Tennyson gave, but (which was unreasonable) to complain of him because he did not give those other things.
The young critics of that time, or the more ferocious of
them, went so far as to assert that he was not a poet at all.
That depreciation is passing ; its violence is already past.
It has been of no little service in making us revise our
traditional judgments and examine their foundations ; it
makes us test and discriminate, and so enables us to see
more clearly what he really was, and is.

He was a poet : and he was a poet from first to last
throughout his long life.   His earliest publication was in
1827, his last volume was in print, but not actually
published, at his death in 1892.   This long productive
period of sixty-five years is almost unexampled ; and
some of his finest work was produced at the end of his
life.   We are apt to think of poetry as a thing belonging
to youth ; but there is a second youth, as well as the more
ordinary second childhood, for those who in the course
of life have not dried up or liquefied.   If Milton had
died at fifty, he would be known as one who wrote some
wonderful poetry in his youth and then ceased to be a
poet at all.

The long period of Tennyson's poetical life is the more
impressive because it followed a group of great poets
who died young.   Within the four years 1821 to 1824,
Keats died at twenty-five, Shelley at thirty, Byron at
thirty-six.   Wordsworth long survived his own poetical

powers ; nearly all his first-rate poetry, that in virtue of
which he lives, had been written when he was under forty.
The amazing poetical genius of Coleridge only worked for
some half-dozen years.   Light after light had gone out.
The throne of English poetry was in effect vacant when
Tennyson stepped into it.   Other poets followed ; other
schools of poetry rose and fell.   But so long as Tennyson
lived, no one seriously thought of dethroning him.   The
volume of his output going on and on produced a cumu-
lative, even to some extent, it might be said, a hypnotic
effect.   The analogy in this respect between him and
Queen Victoria makes his position as the typical Victorian
poet the more striking.   He started ten years ahead of
her, and thenceforward the two kept pace at an even
distance ; his poetical life was, as remarked above, from
1827 to 1892, her reign from 1837 to 1901.   Both
opened a new age, with the advantage of youth on their
side.   Both passed through a long middle period of
imperfect success, with intervals of what may almost be
called eclipse.   Both went steadily on their own way ;
they wore down criticism, they conquered popularity by
the strength of their appeal to common feelings and
instincts.   Both at last became an institution ; so much
so that their disappearance gave a shock as though of
sudden disappearance of the old landmarks and entrance
into a changed world.

   Tennyson was Poet Laureate for forty-two years.   The
Laureateship came to him by a lucky accident : but he
was always lucky.   Five years before, he had a similar
stroke of luck when he received a Civil List pension of
£200 a year.   It was got for him by Monckton Milnes
(Lord Houghton) from Peel, who was then Prime
Minister, at the insistence of Carlyle.   The story is well
known how, when Milnes objected that his constituents

would be very angry about this, Carlyle observed, " On the Day of Judgment, when the Lord asks you why you didn't get that pension for Alfred Tennyson, it won't do to lay the blame on your constituents ; it is you that will be damned." The impression that had been produced on Carlyle by the *Poems* of 1842 has been imperishably recorded by him in words which are equally familiar, but which will bear repetition.

Truly [he wrote to Tennyson after reading them], it is long since in any English Book, Poetry or Prose, I have felt the pulse of a real man's heart as I do in this same. A right valiant, true fighting, victorious heart ; strong as a lion's, yet gentle, loving, and full of music : what I call a genuine singer's heart ! There are tones as of the nightingale ; low murmurs as of wood-doves at summer noon ; everywhere a noble sound as of the free winds and leafy woods. The sunniest glow of Life dwells in that soul, chequered duly with dark streaks from night and Hades : everywhere one feels as if all were fill'd with yellow glowing sunlight, some glorious golden Vapour ; from which form after form bodies itself ; naturally, *golden* forms. In one word, there seems to be a note of " The Eternal Melodies " in this man ; for which let all other men be thankful and joyful ! . . . This is not babble, it is speech ; true deposition of a volunteer witness. And so I say let us all rejoice somewhat. And so let us all smite rhythmically, all in concert, " the sounding furrows " ; and sail forward with new cheer, " beyond the sunset," whither we are bound :

> " It may be that the gulfs will wash us down,
> It may be we shall touch the happy Isles
> And see the great Achilles whom we knew ! "

These lines do not make me weep, but there is in me what would fill whole Lachrymatories as I read. But do you, when you return to London, come down to me and let us smoke a pipe together. With few words, with many, or with none, it need not be an ineloquent Pipe !

Such as he had been from the beginning, and was then, such he remained to the end : very simple, very shy, with something about him that without any strain or self-consciousness gave the feeling of his being bigger than other men and living on a different plane. He produced this effect on the circle of his Cambridge contemporaries. They idolised him, and he accepted their idolatry, but took no pains to justify it, or to make any return to them for it. To them he was like a young god (the Hyperion of Edward FitzGerald) ; giving a sense of effortless power in all he said and did, but induced with difficulty to say much or to do anything. Fame, wealth, rank, all came to him later, but came for the most part unsought. He never flattered and never advertised. Like Shakespeare, he might have said of himself, " I am that I am " ; and he would have been very ready to continue the quotation, " and they that level at my offences reckon up their own." Much of his best poetry, so he said, and one cannot doubt his sincerity or question his judgment, was irreparably lost because he could not bring himself to face the effort of writing it down. Yet, by all accounts, he was a remarkably good man of business, particularly in his dealings with publishers. He always absolutely refused to have any occupation but poetry ; and by poetry alone he acquired not only fame but fortune.

He came of a remarkable stock. He was one of twelve children, all of whom but two lived to be over seventy, and several of whom were decidedly queer—as indeed he was himself. His father, a man of brilliant gifts clouded by fits of melancholia, died when Tennyson was an undergraduate at Cambridge. His mother, who seems to have been in a different way equally remarkable, lived to a great age, retaining to the last the innocence and soft-heartedness—" you whose light-blue eyes are tender over drowning flies "—of her girlhood, and an attractiveness which was irresistible.

At Cambridge, he found himself among a group of

young men of very varied and remarkable ability.   They included Edward FitzGerald and Richard Monckton Milnes ; R. C. Trench and James Spedding ; J. M. Kemble, the founder in this country of the scientific study of Early English ; and Arthur Hallam, to whom Tennyson gave all and more than all the admiring devotion which he himself received from the other members of the circle.   Hallam was the only one among them whom he regarded as his superior—one might say, as his better angel—and who had a real influence over him.   How profound and how permanent that influence was, need not be recalled ; his sudden death in 1833 left a lasting mark on Tennyson's life.   Not *In Memoriam* alone, but nearly the whole body of his poetry bears that indelible mark.

Just fifty years after Hallam's death, another famous contemporary, and a friend both of his and of Tennyson's, drew an interesting contrast between the spheres in which the poet and the statesman exercise their function.   In September 1883 Mr. Gladstone, then Prime Minister, spoke in acknowledgment of the freedom of the burgh of Kirkwall which had been conferred on Tennyson and himself in the course of a pleasure-voyage in the North Sea.

Mr. Tennyson's exertions [he said] have been on a higher plane of human action than mine.   He has worked in a higher field, and his work will be more durable.   In distant times, some may ask with regard to the Prime Minister, Who was he ? and what did he do ? we know nothing about him.   But the Poet Laureate has written his own song on the hearts of his countrymen that can never die.   Time is powerless against him.

It was a tribute to poetry, which the speaker, no doubt, thought a splendid one.   How far was it true ?   To call time powerless against anything of human origin may be a rhetorical exaggeration.   Horace and Virgil, nineteen hundred years earlier, had claimed for their poems a life as long as the dominion of Rome ; Horace with quiet certainty, Virgil with that uncertain wistfulness in which he stands apart from all other poets. It has been longer ; it still persists unimpaired. Were Tennyson's to last as long, his claim to be one of the immortals could hardly be disputed. Forty years—only one generation—have already made Gladstone's figure a little dim. Tennyson's fame is not the same as it once was, but two elements in it stand secure. Historically, he is the voice of a past and a very remarkable age, and thus of perpetual and even increasing interest to those who realise the continuity of history, and the continuity of the poetry in which history is illuminated and interpreted. But, further, in his best work he lives now and will continue to live. Criticism on the one hand, a new perspective on the other, have enabled us to distinguish. Much of his poetry is mannered and laboured ; some is commonplace ; not a little has been pronounced, by common consent, a failure. If we allow all this, it remains none the less true that in the lyric and the elegy he reaches supreme excellence ; that he raised the standard of craftsmanship for English poetry ; and that his mastery of phrase, both in melody and in delicate accuracy, is endlessly astonishing. His manner, because it came so near being a mannerism, was easy to parody : but all attempts at serious imitation of the manner are flat and poor ; they lack the authentic tone.

Let us then try to discriminate. In order to do so, it is as well to set aside a good deal, alike in his early and immature poetry ; in a long middle period during which inspiration dwindled, and the laborious perfection of execution failed to redeem a certain lack of vital substance; and in the autumnal fruitage which, while it includes some of his greatest masterpieces, is very diverse in quality. Poets are misjudged if they are judged by their inferior work. Wordsworth can be flat, Keats can be vulgar, Shelley can be nebulous. That is not what matters ; nor does it touch their real greatness.

The volumes of 1830 and 1833 revealed a new voice in poetry, and the beginning of an era. They are Tennyson in germ ; they display nearly all his excellences, and all his faults. Among these are a provincialism which he never wholly outgrew, and which bars his claim to be one of the great world-poets ; a sentimentality which he shared with his age and did much to intensify ; an amount of bad taste which would be fatal but for its conjunction with imagination and genius. He is fingering the instrument of poetry with a touch still uncertain ; some of these early poems he afterwards suppressed, others he altered so much that they were practically rewritten. But already he can draw out of his instrument tones and harmonies hitherto unknown. Three pieces may be singled out as in this respect specially interesting.

The first of these is the lyric of two stanzas (to which he gave no title) beginning *My life is full of weary days*. It is a sort of prevision of *In Memoriam*, of which it is in some sense the germ. But it is further remarkable as one of the few lyrics, since the singing-age of the sixteenth and earlier seventeenth century, which are faultless, which unite perfect simplicity with high specific distinction. That is true of it in its later form ; for he greatly altered it after its first appearance, and what is perhaps unusual, all the alterations are improvements. It is one instance out of a good many, of a poem or a passage in a poem where the wording and phrasing seem the immediate product of an almost literal inspiration, but where we know as a fact that they come of minute and even laborious revision ; as, to take one celebrated case, with the three forms through which Keats'

Not so much air as on a summer's day
Robs not one light seed from the feathered grass

passed before it took its actual and seemingly effortless perfection.

The second is *Mariana in the Moated Grange*, with its strange power of making familiar things to be as if they were not familiar ; the criterion or definition, as may be remembered, laid down by Shelley for poetry itself. With it must be taken its companion-piece, the hardly less magical *Mariana in the South*. This, unlike the other, in which he only made one very slight change, was almost rewritten by him later ; and was not, we may be disposed to think, improved in the writing. In the later and familiar version, beautiful as it is, there is nothing that equals, for vivid and intimate realisation, the opening stanza of the earlier :

Behind the barren hill unsprung
    With pointed rocks against the light
The crag sharp-shadowed overhung
    Each glaring creek and inlet bright.
Far, far, one light blue ridge was seen
    Looming like baseless fairyland :
    Eastward a slip of burning sand
Dark-rimmed with sea, and bare of green.
Down in the dry salt marshes stood
    That house dark-latticed. Not a breath
    Swayed the sick vineyard underneath
Or moved the dusty southernwood.[1]

It is the first entrance in his poetry of the non-English element which thereafter appears intermittently, and but seldom, as in his fits of longing for " the palms and temples of the South," in which he had been anticipated

---

[1] I have not retained the original typography by which Tennyson had compound epithets like *dark-rimmed* printed as single words. It only checks the reader's eye ; and he himself afterwards condemned it as an affectation.

by so different a poet as Pope, or in the wistful sentence
in a letter written when he was thirty, prophetically true
as it turned out, " I shall never see the Eternal City, nor
that dome, the wonder of the world."

Most remarkable of the three, and quite unique either
in his work or in that of any other, is the *Hesperides*, the
song heard by the Phoenician Hanno on his circum-
navigation of Africa.   It takes up the romantic movement
at its intensest, just at the point where Keats had left it.
Tennyson suppressed the poem and never allowed it to
be republished ; until it was reprinted in his Life it
remained, except to a few, practically unknown.   Full as
it is of beauties, it is so continuous a symphonic structure
that it could only suffer from fragmentary quotation.
It must be read and appreciated as a whole ; and with
it may well be read the song of the Hesperides in Morris'
Life and Death of Jason, the lyric beginning

O ye who to this place have strayed
That never for man's eyes was made.

That is equally exquisite in its beauty, but wholly distinct
in its clear gem-like precision, its lucid simplicity, from
the " huge cloudy symbols of a high romance " which
never perhaps before except in Keats, and never again since,
have received so magical an embodiment as in this poem
of Tennyson's.   When both these are read, there should
be read likewise the passage in the epilogue to Milton's
Comus, which is in some sense the germ of both.   There,
in a few perfect words (they were prefixed by Tennyson
to his own poem) the romantic motive is treated in the
classic spirit and with the classic reticence.   Among
them, the three treatments of the single motive give keys
to the whole evolution of English poetry, fixed points of
achievement from which bearings may be taken.

Why did Tennyson suppress the *Hesperides* ?   Was he

frightened of pursuing this exciting and splendid path? Did his Cambridge friends and critics, perhaps, disapprove of it? it may well have gone over their heads : or did he feel, himself, that this was a note almost beyond his compass? There is no evidence. At all events we find him moving in the other direction ; not liberating imagination, but harnessing it, and bestowing infinite labour on technical finish. That is the period of some of his most perfect and most universally familiar poems. It is the period of *The Lady of Shalott* and *Oenone*, both of which were later remodelled to their great advantage. It is the period of *The Lotos Eaters*, a poem full of beauties, but, after the exquisite opening, not on the same level as the *Hesperides* except for its one supreme stanza :

Lo ! in the middle of the wood
The folded leaf is wooed from out the bud
With winds upon the branch, and there
Grows green and broad, and takes no care,
Sun-steeped at noon, and in the moon
Nightly dew-fed ; and turning yellow
Falls, and floats adown the air.
Lo ! sweetened with the summer light
The full-juiced apple, waxing over-mellow,
Drops in a silent autumn night.
All its allotted length of days
The flower ripens in its place,
Ripens and fades, and falls, and hath no toil,
Fast-rooted in the fruitful soil.

It is the period of the *Palace of Art* and the *Dream of Fair Women*, with their gorgeous and rather overloaded enrichment ; and written about the same time, though not published until much later, of three masterpieces which are beyond criticism, the *Ulysses* and *Tithonus* of 1834, and the lyric *O that 'twere possible*, around which by long expansions and accretions grew the dramatic monologue of *Maud*.

He was taking soundings everywhere in the ocean of poetry ; particularly in two regions, the English idylls which brought him his first large popularity, and the Arthurian legend which continued for many years, indeed all through his life, to dominate his imagination. *The Idylls of the King* will have to be mentioned later ; but the *Morte d'Arthur*, long afterwards incorporated in them bodily, stands by itself and is a classic.   There is a pretty story of Tennyson while the *Morte d'Arthur* was in gestation, in a boat on Windermere with Edward FitzGerald, coming out in his deep voice with the lines,

> Nine years she wrought it, sitting in the deeps
> Upon the hidden bases of the hills,

and simply adding, " Not bad, that, Fitz, is it ? "   He was sounding in many deeps.

It was a few years later that Carlyle—unequalled in the art of portraiture except perhaps by Mrs. Carlyle, who unfortunately left no companion picture from her own hand—wrote of him :

A fine, large-featured, dim-eyed, bronze-coloured, shaggy-headed man is Alfred : dusty, smoky, free and easy : who swims outwardly and inwardly with great composure in an articulate element as of tranquil chaos and tobacco-smoke : great now and then when he does emerge : a most restful, brotherly, solid-hearted man.

The truth of the epithets here is wonderful.   Such he remained until the end, except that the shaggy head had grown bald, showing the high dome familiar from portraits.   Such he was two months before his death, at Aldworth.   That is little more than thirty years ago ; yet to recall it seems to be a backward look upon a very distant past.

Out of that tranquil chaos he emerged into wide recognition with the two volumes of *Poems* of 1842.   In these most of the earlier poems were included, and many others were added, several of which are notable not merely on their own account but also as typical of the divergent manners in which he was experimenting. *The Gardener's Daughter* opens his middle period of the highly-elaborated and heavily-adorned treatment of comparatively slight subjects drawn from modern life, carried on by him later in *Aylmer's Field, Enoch Arden*, and many other pieces. These were greatly admired by their immediate audience, and retained their popularity long ; now they seem, perhaps, a little faded and devitalised ; it is not on them, at all events, that his claim to immortality could be based. *The Talking Oak*, which bears some analogy to them, is an attempt, not by any means unsuccessful, to raise familiar verse to a higher plane by adroit handling and perfect finish of workmanship. Into *Locksley Hall* he poured the whole spirit of the age, with its passionate mixture of hope—" hope wide of eye and wild of wing "—and of discontent. Each age has its own discontents and its own hopes ; and it is difficult now to realise, and impossible to recapture, the attitude of mind which made *Locksley Hall* for a time to many ardent souls something like a new gospel. Among the new lyrics in these volumes were the *Edward Gray*, a lyrical ballad in which Tennyson claimed that he had, if but for once, attained true simplicity ; the *St. Agnes' Eve*, where religious mysticism is remarkably combined with precision of drawing and sharpness of edge ; and the famed *Break, break, break*, four stanzas which, in a few simple words, gave a new power to language and, it might also be said, a new interpretation of life. If poetry could be weighed against poetry—as it cannot—it might be said that this single lyric, composed, it is pleasant to remember, in a Lincolnshire lane at five o'clock on a summer morning, was equivalent to the whole of *In Memoriam*. It sums up, in some sense, the whole of his earlier poetry as *Crossing the Bar* sums up the whole work of his life.

Here the earlier period comes to an end. He had made good with the older generation. Wordsworth had already said of him, " He is decidedly the first of our living poets." Rogers, the last inheritor of a tradition still more remote, had said of *Locksley Hall*, " Shakespeare could not have done it better." And, while to the larger reading public he was still only one name among others, and not one of the popular favourites in any wide sense, many of the younger generation which was already growing up regarded him with an admiration almost amounting to idolatry.

The division between the two halves of his life comes in 1850 and is marked with unusual sharpness. In May of that year he published *In Memoriam* ; in June he married ; in November he succeeded Wordsworth in the Laureateship. This last incident was the immediate occasion of his dedicatory verses *To the Queen*, prefixed to the new issue of his collected poems in the following March. The Exhibition of 1851 was then in preparation, and was hoped or imagined to inaugurate a new era not only for the nation but for the world.

> She brought a vast design to pass
>   When Europe and the scattered ends
>   Of our fierce world were mixt as friends
> And brethren in her halls of glass.
>
> And statesmen at her Council met
>   Who knew the seasons when to take
>   Occasion by the hand, and make
> The bounds of freedom wider yet.

In somewhat a similar spirit, Tennyson was now setting himself to extend the bounds of his own poetry, and to write on a larger scale. But he was essentially a lyric and idyllic artist. His longest poems are, generally speaking, his least successful. His descriptive faculty was unsurpassed, but he had not the narrative gift, and so his narrative poems tend to lose themselves in masses of description. *Enoch Arden* takes nearly a thousand lines to tell a story suitable for a hundred or a hundred and fifty. Nothing could be finer than the ornament, only there is far too much of it. *The Princess*, which is also loaded with minor felicities, received from Tennyson himself the sub-title of " a medley," and has probably never been regarded otherwise than as an elaborate failure. *In Memoriam* is, as he himself calls it, a linked series of " short swallow-flights of song." Its fortunes were very remarkable. At first it attracted little attention. But its power of giving crystallised expression to thoughts, doubts, beliefs, aspirations which were stirring in thousands of minds grew steadily on an increasing audience. To many, and in particular to earnest people who wished to think but liked their thinking done for them, who clung to conservatism yet had a longing to be progressive, it became a sort of bible. In the seventies there was probably hardly a pulpit in England from which it was not habitually quoted ; to such strange uses was Pope's criterion " What oft was thought, but ne'er so well expressed " turned. Scores of lines and stanzas in it became part of the common consciousness of the English-speaking world.

After *In Memoriam* there was a long pause in Tennyson's production, and a curious temporary set-back in public appreciation of his work. While *In Memoriam* itself was slowly but surely finding acceptance, the masterpiece of *Maud*, five years later, was received with a disconcerting lack of intelligence ; it might be better to say at once, with blank stupidity. The application of the lyrical gift to a dramatic, as previously to a philosophico-religious, subject matter had as it seemed failed ; and the seeming failure caused him great discouragement. There was another long interval ; and then he broke fresh ground. The publication in 1859 of the first four *Idylls of the King* (*Enid, Vivien, Elaine, Guinevere*) created an instant revolution ; it opened the epoch of his national popularity. Ten thousand copies of this volume were sold in the first week.

Of these four Idylls, as of the whole cycle of twelve into which they finally grew, it is difficult even now to be sure whether they will perish from their weakness of structure, their conventionality of thought, their over-elaboration of minute detail and metrical artifice, or will be saved by, and for the sake of, their lovely ornament. That they can ever regain their first reputation (though it is never safe to prophesy unless you know) may be thought impossible. It is no less certain that lines and phrases and passages in them are as imperishable as the English language. To understand what they meant at the time, it may be sufficient to quote two contemporary criticisms. One is the Prince Consort's : the period which we are now considering might be called the Albertine age ; there was a Victorian age before it, and another after it. " They quite rekindle," Prince Albert wrote to Tennyson, " the feeling with which the legends of King Arthur must have inspired the chivalry of old, whilst the graceful form in which they are presented blends those feelings with the softer tone of our present age." Comment on the words would be superfluous. The other is that of Ruskin, who was himself essentially a Victorian, but who had a spiritual instinct entirely his own. " I feel," he wrote, with that delicate courtesy which was the

most beautiful feature in his character, " the art and finish
in these poems a little more than I like to feel it."

The year before, a little volume of poems, which has
now long been recognised as marking a new dawn in
poetry, had crept unnoticed into the world. It is startling
to read *The Defence of Guinevere* and *King Arthur's Tomb*,
with their marvellous " perception and experience," in
Swinburne's admirable words, " of tragic truth, of subtle
and noble, terrible and piteous things," their " touch of
passion at once so broad and so sure," and to realise that
they are earlier in date than Tennyson's *Guinevere*.
A few years later came the epoch-making *Atalanta in
Calydon*. Browning too was coming by his own ; and
in 1870 the publication of Rossetti's *Poems and Ballads*
shifted the axis of English poetry. With the later Idylls
(four more in 1869, two more in 1872), it really began
to look as if Tennyson's day were over. His mannerisms
had become confirmed. He was casting about (as may
be read in his Life) for subjects : which in poetry as in
all art means sickness, if not death. There is a widely
circulated story, the authenticity of which is, however,
very doubtful, of his having been heard to say, half to
himself and as it were thinking aloud, " I can execute
like Shakespeare, and I have nothing to say." Whether
or not he ever said this or something like this, it embodies
a half-truth. He could not execute like Shakespeare ;
of no one, except just here and there for a moment, can
that be said ; but he could execute like Tennyson, which
is praise enough. And he still had something to say,
which he said, and which is beyond praise.

That is not to be found in the series of dramas, from
the *Queen Mary* of 1875 onwards, on which he spent
much labour, with inadequate result, for a good many
years. He had not the dramatic, any more than he had

the narrative, gift. It is perhaps one which is innate rather than acquired. But his own life was throughout unusually shut off from professional activities and practical affairs. As a critic of the drama he is said to have been extraordinarily fine and illuminative ; but there is a long step from that to its concrete handling. Of his acted dramas, only *Becket* was successful on the stage ; it was produced after his death, and owed its success in large measure to what may be called the lyrical genius of Irving. To produce plays like Shakespeare's a dramatist must not only have a genius comparable to his, but live a life like his, be steeped in the atmosphere of the theatre, have the receptive and assimilative faculties highly developed and give them free play. Tennyson was naturally brooding and moody ; " I cannot write except in the mood," he said of himself. The first line of *The Revenge* lay in his desk for years ; then the mood came, and the whole poem was composed in a day or two. When still at Cambridge, he wrote what must have been equal to anything he ever wrote, " a poem on Lancelot and Guinevere." It is wholly lost except for one verse preserved by FitzGerald :

Life of the life within my blood,
  Light of the light within mine eyes,
The May begins to breathe and bud
  And softly blow the balmy skies.
Bathe with me in the fiery flood
  And mingle kisses, tears and sighs,
Life of the life within my blood,
  Light of the light within mine eyes.

Many years later, the substance of these lines (if one can speak intelligibly of the substance of a lyric) reappeared as the Song of Vivien in the *Idylls*, but re-cast, and with the enchantment gone out of it. And later, he composed a poem on Lancelot and the Grail, " as good verses as I ever wrote "—the words this time are his own—which he never committed to paper at all. These are only instances of many others, " blown up the chimney with my pipe-smoke, or written and thrown into the fire."

But with all his moods and whims, with all the mannerisms which he will not allow us to forget, with all that early-Victorian bad taste into which even in his maturity he would relapse, he was true to poetry ; and poetry—*amor che a nullo amato amar perdona*—was true to him. Constantly he kept breaking out into some miraculous new flower of lyric : each, it may be, repeating some motive already handled, but each making a direct and separate appeal.

> And murmurs of a deeper voice
>   Going before to some far shrine
> Teach that still heart the stronger choice
>   Till all thy life one way incline
>   With one wide will that closes thine.
>
> And when the zoning eve has died
>   Where yon dark valleys wind forlorn,
> Come Hope and Memory, spouse and bride,
>   From out the borders of the morn,
>   With that fair child between them born.
>
> And when no mortal motion jars
>   The blackness round the tombing sod,
> Through silence and the trembling stars
>   Comes Faith from tracts no feet have trod,
>   And Virtue, like a household god
>
> Promising empire : such as those
>   Once heard at dead of night to greet
> Troy's wandering prince, so that he rose
>   With sacrifice, while all the fleet
>   Had rest by stony hills of Crete.

After the long and rather sultry afternoon there followed an evening of incomparable beauty. The lyrics of these last years, if they have not the fragile and irrecoverable charm of a spring flowerage, yield an even richer music, and are written with the ease of complete mastery. This is true alike of those where the rhythms are simple and the words seem to fall into their places as it were by accident, and of those prolonged and gorgeous rhythmical devices with which they are counterchanged. Both are unequalled ; both, it may be said, are unsurpassable. Take, on the one hand, such verses as these :

> Like would-be guests an hour too late
>   Who down the pathway moving on
> With easy laughter find the gate
>   Is bolted and the master gone :

or

> O rose tree planted in my grief
>   And growing on her tomb,
> Her dust is greening in your leaf,
>   Her blood is in your bloom :

or

> The silver year should cease to mourn and sigh—
>   Not long to wait—
> So close are we, dear Mary, you and I
>   To that dim gate ;

where the old brooding over life and death is resumed and etherealised ; or, on the other hand, such a lyric as the *Early Spring*, the one beginning

> Once more the heavenly power
>   Makes all things new,

with its wonderful sense of the self-renewing power of life : what in both kinds is remarkable is the delicacy and certainty of the touch, the smoothness of the mechanism, so complete that it does not seem to be mechanism at all.

No less admirable is the effortless perfection of work-

manship in the long rolling cadence of the lyrics in which,
towards the end of his life, he made the last, and one of
the greatest, of his metrical achievements, and gave new
wings to the soaring flight of verse : *Vastness* ; the lines
To Virgil, which are perhaps the highest tribute ever paid
by one poet to another, and in which there sounds the
ocean-roll of " the stateliest measure ever moulded by
the life of man," the incomparable Virgilian hexameter ;
and alongside of these, the two stanzas entitled *God and
the Universe* which sum up, in a concentrated form, his
final attitude towards the great mysteries over which he
had brooded all his life long.   They may well be quoted
here.

> Will my tiny spark of being wholly vanish in your depths and
>   heights ?
> Must my day be dark by reason, O ye heavens, of your boundless
>   nights,
> Rush of suns, and roll of systems, and your fiery clash of
>   meteorites ?
>
> Spirit, nearing yon dark portal at the limit of thy human state,
> Fear not thou the hidden purpose of that Power which alone
>   is great,
> Nor the myriad world, His Shadow, nor the silent Opener of
>   the Gate.

Of *Crossing the Bar*, which he wished to be regarded
as his last word, it is needless to speak.   " It came in a
moment," when he was eighty, and with the same instan-
taneous completeness was taken at once to the heart of
the world, and became, one might say, part of the universal
language.   Consummate metrical and verbal artifice has
in it reached its final goal and is indistinguishable from
the most direct simplicity :

> that art
> Which, you say, adds to Nature, is an art
> That Nature makes.

Such art does not yield its secret ; it cannot be either analysed or imitated : but it is worth pointing out what few, perhaps, of the countless readers of *Crossing the Bar* have noticed, that the metrical structure of all four stanzas is different, and that the subtle interlinking of rhythms thus produced is part at least, though a small part, of the secret.

In constructional power, whether as it manifests itself in the conduct of a " great argument " or in the periodic movement of vast rhythms, Tennyson does not stand in the first rank ; he is not comparable to Milton or Shelley, perhaps not to a number of other and lesser English poets. He works, on this large scale, by minute accumulated touches ; his elaboration of ornament is often felt to be tedious, his perpetual variations of metre, in his long blank-verse poems like the *Idylls of the King*, to be fretful and to impede the amplitude which that noble metre should possess.   But even in the periods during which his inspiration seems to flag and his mannerisms to become uncomfortably prominent, we shall find here and there the authentic note of his genius reasserting itself in full.

We who are the survivors of the Tennysonian age, and have seen the revolt against Tennysonianism grow up, culminate, and fade, are hardly perhaps in a position to sum up his poetical achievement or to estimate either its quantity or its quality as it may appear to those who approach it with minds free from the entanglements of tradition and association.   That it was great, there can be no doubt.   Whether we regard him as a master of metrical and verbal felicities ; as an interpreter of Nature with unsurpassed and in some ways unequalled delicacy and accuracy ; as the articulate voice of an age from which the newer world inherits directly, and the greatness of which, no less than its limitations, we are only now beginning to realise ; or, which is the conclusion of the whole matter, as one who gave a new music to language and to life, his place is assured among the English Classics, among the poets whose poetry is the permanent heritage of the whole English-speaking people.